STUDENT UNIT GUIDE

NEW EDITION

Edexcel A2 Economics Unit 4

The Global Economy

Quintin Brewer

Philip Allan Updates, an imprint of Hodder Education, an Hachette UK company, Market Place, Deddington, Oxfordshire, OX15 0SE

Orders
Bookpoint Ltd, 130 Milton Park, Abingdon, Oxfordshire, OX14 4SB
tel: 01235 827827
fax: 01235 400401
e-mail: education@bookpoint.co.uk
Lines are open 9.00 a.m.–5.00 p.m., Monday to Saturday, with a 24-hour message answering service. You can also order through the Philip Allan Updates website: www.philipallan.co.uk

© Quintin Brewer 2012

ISBN 978-1-4441-4791-9

First printed 2012
Impression number 5 4
Year 2017 2016 2015 2014 2013

Cover picture: James Steidl/Fotolia

Typeset by Integra, India

Printed in Dubai

Hachette UK's policy is to use papers that are natural, renewable and recyclable products and made from wood grown in sustainable forests. The logging and manufacturing processes are expected to conform to the environmental regulations of the country of origin.

Contents

Content Guidance

Questions & Answers

Getting the most from this book

Examiner tips

Advice from the examiner on key points in the text to help you learn and recall unit content, avoid pitfalls, and polish your exam technique in order to boost your grade.

Knowledge check

Rapid-fire questions throughout the Content Guidance section to check your understanding.

Knowledge check answers

1   Turn to the back of the book for the Knowledge check answers.

Summary

Summaries

● Each core topic is rounded off by a bullet-list summary for quick-check reference of what you need to know.

Questions & Answers

Exam-style questions

Examiner comments on the questions
Tips on what you need to do to gain full marks, indicated by the icon 🄔.

Sample student answers
Practise the questions, then look at the student answers that follow each set of questions.

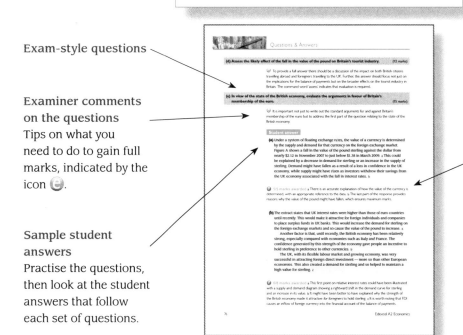

Examiner commentary on sample student answers
Find out how many marks each answer would be awarded in the exam and then read the examiner comments (preceded by the icon 🄔) following each student answer. Annotations that link back to points made in the student answers show exactly how and where marks are gained or lost.

About this book

This guide has been written to prepare students for Unit 4 of Edexcel's GCE A-level examination in Economics: The Global Economy. It provides an overview of the knowledge and skills required for the examination in the 'Global Economy'. This unit is synoptic, which implies that knowledge and understanding of the material covered in previous units is required. You should consider the possibilities of using both microeconomic and macroeconomic concepts from previous units in answering questions. The main areas covered in this unit include macroeconomic objectives and policies; public finance; globalisation; free trade and protectionism; the balance of payments and exchange rates; the constraints of economic growth and development; strategies to achieve economic growth and development.

This guide is aimed at developing the skills and knowledge that you have gained over the whole course, as well as covering the material new to this unit. It should be used alongside your own notes and other revision aids. Inevitably it includes only brief summaries of the key areas.

The Content Guidance section provides an overview of the main topics with reference to the theoretical requirements of the unit. It also identifies the synoptic elements covered in previous units.

The final part of the guide provides questions and answers on the topics covered in Unit 4. There are two essays and two data–response questions, with a selection of student answers. These are annotated with examiner's comments, identifying both the good and weaker aspects of the responses. These should help you to understand the expectations you are required to fulfil for a high grade. After reviewing this unit, you should attempt the questions under timed conditions and then compare your answers with those provided in the guide. This will enable you to identify areas where further revision is required.

Content Guidance

This section focuses on the key elements relating to the global economy. It starts with a reconsideration of macroeconomic objectives and policies, an area first studied in Unit 2. However, for Unit 4 you need to consider these topics in a global context. Given the increasing interdependence of economies, economic events in one country impact on others and similarly economic policies adopted by one country affect others.

The next section considers the main elements of public finance: public expenditure, taxation and public sector borrowing. Although the emphasis is on the UK in this section, international comparisons should also be made.

The third section covers globalisation, its causes, costs and benefits. It also includes free trade and protectionism. This is followed by an examination of the balance of payments accounts and exchange rates. This is an area in which global imbalances may be considered and their implications for exchange rates. Following this, there is a consideration of the meaning of, and measurement and factors influencing, international competitiveness, together with a consideration of how it might be improved.

There is then a section on poverty and inequality as a prelude to an examination of the limits to growth and development. Finally, strategies to promote growth and development are discussed, with the focus primarily on developing countries.

Macroeconomic objectives and policy

Unit 4 is synoptic so it is highly appropriate that this topic should be revisited after being introduced in Unit 2. While much of the material will be familiar, a more evaluative approach is required in Unit 4, as is the need to consider macroeconomic objectives and policy in an international setting. Given the global imbalances which arose prior to the credit crunch, a review of macroeconomic objectives in a global context is important.

Similarly, the turbulent international economic situation in 2008 and 2009 has led to a re-evaluation of the effectiveness of the tools of macroeconomic policy in achieving macroeconomic objectives. For example, the limitations of interest rate policy were exposed as the global economy headed for a serious downturn in 2008–09.

Objectives of macroeconomic policy

In a global context, it is worth remembering that different countries may place rather different emphases on their priorities. Nevertheless, the following goals are usually included:

- **Economic growth.** An increase in real GDP is often regarded as the fundamental objective of macroeconomic policy by governments, not only in poor developing countries, where it is seen as a means of reducing absolute poverty, but also in developed economies by governments wishing to maintain popularity. Further, many economists regard this objective as being pivotal in achieving the other macroeconomic objectives.

- **Sustainable growth.** This is usually defined as the ability to meet the needs of the present generation without compromising the needs of future generations. There have been growing concerns that rapid economic growth in countries such as China and India is unsustainable in terms of the environment and the rapid depletion of natural resources. The limitation of the **external costs** associated with economic growth is an objective that can only be met with global cooperation.

- **A low and stable inflation rate.** Apart from other disadvantages, high inflation rates can damage the international competitiveness of a country's goods, so most countries pursue policies designed to maintain a low and stable rate of inflation. As equally destructive as high inflation is deflation, which is a sustained fall in the price level: experience from the 1930s suggests that deflation is often associated with depression.

- **Full employment.** This does not mean that every worker is employed, because there will always be frictional unemployment. However, this is usually regarded as being full employment and is referred to as the **natural rate of unemployment**. This objective is most likely to be achieved if there is economic growth.

- **Balance of payments equilibrium on current account.** One of the major imbalances between countries has been in relation to the balance of payments. While the USA and UK have been running large deficits, China has had persistent surpluses. Although the deficits have been financed by inflows into the financial account, many have argued that these are unsustainable in the long term. Huge deficits may result in violent changes in the exchange rate of a country's currency, contributing to instability in the whole economy.

- **Redistribution of income.** Most developed economies used **progressive taxes** and welfare payments, especially means-tested benefits, to redistribute income from the rich to the poor.

- **Fiscal balance.** In the same way that current account deficits may be unsustainable, the same might also be true of large fiscal deficits. This form of imbalance may prove to be a problem if countries are unable to sell government bonds to finance the deficits.

The aggregate-demand/aggregate-supply model

This model, introduced in Unit 2, needs to be covered again so that it can be employed in analysing and evaluating macroeconomic policies and in examining other parts of Unit 4; for example, in considering the impact of an increase in foreign direct investment.

Examiner tip
Remember that this unit is concerned with the global economy, so data on any of the above could relate to any country.

Aggregate demand (*AD*) is the relationship between the quantity of real GDP demanded and the price level. The main components of *AD* are consumption, investment, government expenditure and net exports. Shifts in the *AD* curve may be caused by changes in the following:

- asset prices
- interest rates
- foreign direct investment
- tax rates
- expectations about the future state of the economy
- decisions by the government on its expenditure
- the exchange rate

The Keynesian aggregate supply (AS) curve

For Keynesian economists, the *AS* curve will resemble that shown in Figure 1.

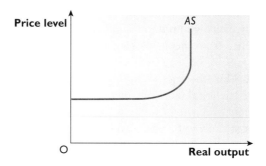

Figure 1 The Keynesian *AS* curve

Keynesians consider that the economy could be in long-run equilibrium at less than the full employment level of real output. At low levels of real output it would be horizontal because there is considerable spare capacity in the economy. As the economy moves towards full employment, bottlenecks in production will occur, along with shortages of some resources, which will push up costs, causing the *AS* curve to rise. At full employment the *AS* curve becomes vertical. Keynesians consider that the economy could be in long-run equilibrium at less than the full employment level of real output, so the Keynesian *AS* curve could be valid in both the short run and long run.

It may be helpful, however, to differentiate between the short-run and long-run *AS* curves, especially for evaluative purposes.

The short-run AS curve

Short-run aggregate supply (*SRAS*) is the relationship between the total quantity of final goods and services supplied (real output) and the price level, holding everything else constant (see Figure 2).

Shifts in the *SRAS* curve may be caused by the following:

- **Changes in wage costs:** an increase in wage rates will raise costs of production and cause the *SRAS* to shift to the left.

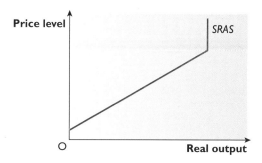

Figure 2 The short-run *AS* curve

- **New legislation:** for example, new health and safety regulations or environmental regulations which increase the costs of firms in the economy would cause the *SRAS* curve to shift to the left.
- **Changes in the prices of raw material and components:** a general fall in commodity prices would cause the *SRAS* to shift to the right.
- **Changes in taxation on firms:** in the UK, employers (as well as employees) are required to pay national insurance contributions. These are really a tax on employment, so if employers' contributions are increased, then the *SRAS* will shift to the left, since costs have increased.

The long-run *AS* curve

Long-run aggregate supply (*LRAS*) is the relationship between the total quantity of final goods and services supplied (real output) and the price level, when there is full employment. According to the neoclassical model, the *LRAS* curve will be vertical, as shown in Figure 3.

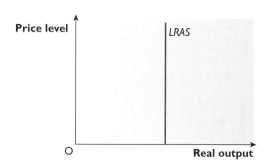

Figure 3 The neoclassical LRAS curve

Shifts in the long-run *AS* curve may be caused by the following factors:

- **Technological change:** new and more efficient methods of production will affect the *LRAS*.
- **The size of the labour force:** this can be influenced both by the natural rate of increase or decrease in the population but also by migration.
- **Human capital:** the skills, knowledge and expertise of the workforce gained through education and training. In turn, this has a significant impact on the productivity of the workforce.

Knowledge check 1

What would be the effect of an increase in oil prices on the price level and real output?

- **Capital stock:** if the capital stock increases relative to the workforce (capital deepening), then productivity should increase.
- **Raw materials:** the discovery of new raw materials will cause the *LRAS* to shift to the right.

Figure 4 shows the equilibrium price level and real output using a Keynesian aggregate-supply curve.

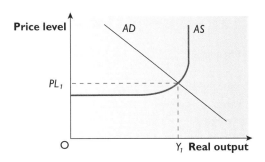

Figure 4 Equilibrium level of real output

Macroeconomic policy instruments

Macroeconomic policies are usually divided into demand-side policies (monetary and fiscal policy) and supply-side policies. For 30 years or so, until the financial crisis of 2008, monetary policy was geared towards the control of inflation while fiscal policy was aimed at achieving the government's fiscal objectives. Supply-side policies were used to secure economic growth and the government's other macroeconomic objectives. In this unit it is important to adopt a critical approach to the effectiveness of these policies.

Monetary policy

Monetary policy refers to the use of interest rates, money supply and exchange rate in order to influence the level of economic activity in a country.

There are various aspects of monetary policy:
- **Inflation targets.** These are used by many countries to maintain a low rate of inflation. In the case of the UK, there is a target of 2% although the rate may vary by up to 1% either side of this, while the European Central Bank has a target of a maximum rate of inflation of 2%. Until 2007, inflation targeting was generally regarded as an effective way of controlling inflation, although countries without targets did not appear to suffer significantly higher rates of inflation. However, following the financial crisis, many economists have argued that an inflation target based on the Consumer Price Index is too narrow. Instead, there should be targets relating to other variables, such as asset prices, in order to prevent asset price 'bubbles' from occurring.
- **Interest rate changes.** These are used to achieve the inflation target, e.g. if the inflation rate is predicted to rise above its target, then the Bank of England increases the base rate. However, the use of interest rates has various disadvantages, e.g. the full effect of an increase in the rate of interest takes between 18 and 24 months to

work through the economy; business costs rise; the exchange rate of the currency may increase, making a country's goods less price competitive.

- **Quantitative easing.** This is sometimes mistakenly referred to as 'printing money'. In practice, it relates to the action of the Central Bank in buying up government bonds and corporate bonds from the commercial banks and other financial institutions. This has the effect of increasing their deposits, thereby giving them the ability to lend more easily to private and business customers. However, some argue that this policy is unlikely to be effective if the banks are risk averse and remain unwilling to lend unless the loan is risk free. There is also the danger that the increased supply of money in the economy could unleash a serious bout of inflation (based on the monetarist belief in the **quantity theory of money**).

  An increase in the money supply could also cause a depreciation in the **exchange rate** which, in turn, would result in an increase in net exports and so increase aggregate demand.

Knowledge check 2

What factors might limit the effectiveness of monetary policy?

Fiscal policy

Fiscal policy refers to the use of government expenditure and taxation in order to influence the level of economic activity in a country. From the 1980s until 2008, its primary role was to ensure stable public finances. However, from 2008 it has once again assumed a role in macroeconomic management not only in the UK but also in China, the USA and a variety of other countries. Some key features of fiscal policy include:

- **Automatic stabilisers:** relate to the fact that some forms of government expenditure and revenues from some taxes change automatically in line with changes in GDP and the state of the economy. These stabilisers help to reduce fluctuations caused by the trade/business cycle. Examples include progressive taxation and welfare payments such as unemployment pay and various means-tested benefits, e.g. pension credits for elderly people living on low incomes.
- **Discretionary fiscal policy:** refers to deliberate changes in taxes and public expenditure designed to achieve the government's macroeconomic objectives. For example, the global economic crisis has led many countries to introduce a 'fiscal stimulus' to prevent severe recession. Typically, these have included increases in public expenditure on infrastructure (roads and bridges in the USA); green technology and targeted subsidies to distressed industries (e.g. the car industry) and tax cuts.

Knowledge check 3

How would public finances be affected by a recession?

Fiscal policy might be effective if the value of the multiplier is high and can have an immediate impact if indirect taxes, such as VAT, are reduced. However, there may be significant time lags. For example, increased government expenditure on investment projects, such as building new hospitals, is unlikely to have an impact for a considerable time because land must be purchased and planning applications approved.

Further, if there is a contractionary fiscal policy in which direct taxes are increased, there could be disincentive effects (e.g. higher corporation tax could reduce investment), while higher income tax rates might reduce incentives to work. It is also difficult to determine the magnitude of changes in public expenditure in advance because the value of the multiplier may not be known.

Supply-side policies

Supply-side policies are a broad range of policies aimed at increasing aggregate supply by increasing competition and increasing incentives. Essentially these are microeconomic policies since they target specific markets, e.g. labour, product or capital markets.

Labour market

Policies aimed at the labour market include:

- **reduction in trade union power:** e.g. making strikes without a secret ballot illegal; making sympathy strikes illegal
- **reduction in unemployment benefits:** which would increase the incentive for unemployed workers to take jobs
- **improvements in human capital:** increased provision and quality of education and training designed to increase the productivity of the workforce
- **reduction in employment protection legislation:** making it easier to hire and fire workers, which contributes to a more flexible workforce
- **reduction in income tax rates:** the aim of these tax cuts is to increase incentives to work and may be analysed using the **Laffer curve** (see page 17).

Product market

Policies aimed at the product market include:

- **privatisation, deregulation and contracting out:**
  - privatisation: involves the sale of state-owned enterprise to the private sector usually through the issue of shares. This policy has been adopted across the globe and in the case of developing countries, privatisation has been a condition for loans given by the International Monetary Fund (IMF).
  - deregulation: when the government removes official barriers to competition. e.g. licences and quality standards
  - contracting out: when parts of services operated by the public sector are put out to tender so that the private sector can compete for the business
- **trade liberalisation:** relates to the removal or reduction in trade barriers and the adoption of policies which allow free capital flows between countries, so making it more attractive for transnational companies to invest in the country
- **promotion of new/small firms:** for example, through tax breaks, short-term loans for new businesses and loan guarantees

Capital market

Policies aimed at the capital market include:

- **deregulation of the financial markets:** such as the reduction of restrictive practices in the city and stock exchange
- **reduction in corporation tax:** or reduction in tax allowances on investment by firms

Criticisms of supply-side policies

Supply-side policies maybe criticised as follows:

- **Increased inequality:** it is argued that they are based on the premise that the rich will work harder if you pay them more and the poor will work harder if you pay them less.
- **Time lags:** some of the measures take a long time to have any impact on the supply side of the economy, e.g. reforms in primary education.
- **The incentive effects of tax cuts may be over-estimated:** in the USA, tax cuts resulted in an increase in labour supply of less than 1%. Similarly, there is little evidence that tax cuts have any significant impact on productivity.
- **Ineffectiveness:** if aggregate demand is low, then these policies may have no effect.
- **Adverse effects of deregulation:** competition might lead to undesirable consequences. For example, the deregulation of financial markets resulted in excessive risk-taking, leading to the near-collapse of the banking system.

Examiner tip
Supply-side policies may be particularly relevant when considering the topic of international competitiveness.

Problems faced by policy makers

Policy makers face a variety of problems when implementing policies to manage the economy. Among these are:

- **Inaccurate information:** for example, information regarding GDP, the balance of payments on current account and retail sales is notoriously inaccurate and subject to subsequent revisions.
- **Risks and uncertainties:** for example, there is considerable uncertainty about the possible impact of quantitative easing. Some monetarist economists argue that it could risk unleashing a massive bout of inflation (because money supply is being increased), while others consider that previous experience in other countries suggests that it will have little effect on the economy.

Summary

- The main objectives of macroeconomic policy include economic growth; sustainability; a low and stable rate of inflation; full employment; balance of payments equilibrium; income redistribution; fiscal balance.
- The AD and AS model should be used not only when discussing policy instruments but throughout this unit where appropriate.
- The short-run AS curve is upward sloping but the long-run AS curve is vertical.
- To achieve the macroeconomic objectives the following policy instruments may be used: monetary; fiscal and supply-side policies.

Examination skills and concepts

- Ability to use the AD/AS model in a variety of contexts (both familiar and unfamiliar).
- Understanding of macroeconomic objectives in a global context, especially that of sustainable growth.
- Ability to evaluate the effectiveness of macroeconomic policy instruments (monetary, fiscal and supply-side policies) in the management of the economy.
- Understanding of the significance of macroeconomic policy in a global context, especially in the light of major global shocks, e.g. the credit crisis.

Common examination errors

- Confusion between the different macroeconomic policy instruments, e.g. between fiscal and supply-side policies.
- Omission of *AD/AS* diagrams and analysis in discussing macroeconomic issues.
- Failure to consider the broader effects of the use of macroeconomic policies, e.g. the impact of interest rate changes on the exchange rates.
- Failure to explain the transmission mechanisms fully.

Linkages with common themes

- Unit 4 builds on the material covered in Unit 2, so it is worth reviewing that unit carefully.
- In particular, you should have a good understanding of demand-side and supply-side policies.

Public finance

There are four elements of public finance which should be considered:
- public expenditure
- taxation
- public sector net borrowing
- public sector net debt

Figure 5 shows the key areas of public finance: public expenditure; taxation; and public sector borrowing, together with various elements of these topics.

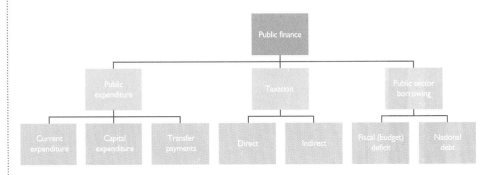

Figure 5 Key aspects of public finance

Public expenditure

Expenditure by central and local government can be categorised into three distinct types:
- **Current expenditure**. This is day-to-day expenditure on goods and services, e.g. salaries of teachers, nurses and drugs used by the NHS.

- **Capital expenditure**. This relates to expenditure on long-term investment projects such as new hospitals and roads.
- **Transfer payments**. These are payments made by the state (from tax revenues) to individuals in the form of benefits for which there is no production in return. Examples include child benefit, state pensions and the jobseekers' allowance.

The objectives of public expenditure include the provision of public goods; defence and internal security; the provision of goods and services which yield external benefits and/or where there may be information gaps and asymmetric information, for example health and education; the redistribution of income; and expenditure to deal with external costs such as pollution, and waste.

Analysis of public expenditure

The following synoptic issues arise when considering public expenditure:
- Given that the amount of public expenditure is likely to be restricted in any one year (e.g. by expected tax revenues), then an increase in expenditure on one area such as education will involve an **opportunity cost** (e.g. new hospitals).
- Increasing expectations relating to healthcare and education are associated with increasing real incomes, so it could be inferred that the demand for these services is **income elastic**.
- An increase in public expenditure represents an injection into the circular flow and so will have a **multiplier effect** on GDP. Not only will aggregate demand increase but expenditure on areas such as education, infrastructure and health might cause an increase in long-run aggregate supply.
- Part of public expenditure might be used for dealing with **external costs**.
- Public expenditure could result in **government failure** (i.e. when intervention by the government results in a net welfare loss).

In addition, there is the issue of crowding out, which might result from increased public expenditure. This might take two forms: resource and financial. Resource crowding out occurs when the economy is operating at full employment and an increase in public expenditure results in insufficient resources being available for the private sector. Financial crowding out occurs when increased public expenditure or tax cuts are financed by increased public sector borrowing, so increasing the demand for loanable funds and driving up interest rates.

The size and pattern of public expenditure

Factors influencing the size and pattern of public expenditure include:
- **The level of GDP:** as incomes increase, the demand for many government-provided services such as health and education rises more than proportionately because demand for them is **income elastic**.
- **The size and age distribution of the population:** an increase in the size of the population (e.g. through immigration) is likely to place extra pressure on public services, while an ageing population will increase demand for medical services and social services for the elderly.
- **Political priorities:** the Labour government placed particular emphasis on improving the quality of health and education services.

Examiner tip

Transfer payments involve redistribution of income. Therefore they are not relevant to the calculation of a country's national income.

Knowledge check 4

What are the two key characteristics of public goods?

Examiner tip

Ensure that you can explain the important synoptic terms in bold: opportunity cost; income elastic demand; multiplier effect; external costs and government failure.

Knowledge check 5

How might financial crowding out affect investment by the private sector?

Examiner tip

When answering questions on this area it is useful to have current knowledge of the reasons for recent changes in the size and pattern of public expenditure.

- **Redistribution of income:** expenditure on those in **relative poverty** (see page 38) and those with disabilities has increased significantly in recent years. For example, there has been an increase in **means-tested benefits** such as family tax credits and pensioners' credits.
- **Discretionary fiscal policy:** the credit crunch has led to the resurrection of fiscal policy as a means of managing the economy.
- **Debt interest:** the massive increase in fiscal deficits from 2008 is leading to sharp rises in the public sector net debt (PSND) (see below). In turn, this will result in higher interest payments on the national debt.

Taxation

Taxes may be divided into two types: direct and indirect. Direct taxes are those levied on income and wealth and the tax burden cannot be passed on to anyone else. Indirect taxes are those levied on expenditure.

The main direct taxes are income tax, corporation tax (on company profits) and capital gains tax, while indirect taxes include VAT, excise duties and tariffs.

Examiner tip

It is important to remember that the distinction between these categories of taxes depends on the relationship between the *percentage* of income paid in tax and taxable income.

There are three broad categories of taxes: progressive, proportional and regressive.
- **A progressive tax** is one in which the proportion of income paid in tax rises as income increases.
- A **proportional tax** is one in which the proportion of income paid in tax remains constant as income increases.
- A **regressive tax** is one in which the proportion of income paid in tax falls as income increases.

Analysing the effects of taxation

When analysing the effects of taxation, the following synoptic issues should be considered:
- An increase in taxes represents a leakage from the circular flow and so would have a downward **multiplier effect** on GDP.
- An increase in indirect tax on a product would cause a leftward shift in the supply curve. The incidence of the tax on consumers and producers depends on the **price elasticity of demand** for the product (see Unit 1).
- Indirect taxes would increase prices above **marginal cost,** so resulting in **allocative inefficiency,** unless **external costs** are associated with the production of the product.
- Indirect taxes might be applied to products that cause external costs.
- An increase in indirect taxes could cause **inflation** via a wage-price spiral. For example, if VAT is increased, prices rise. This could be inflationary if it results in workers demanding higher wages to compensate for the increase in prices.

Knowledge check 6

How would an increase in income tax rates affect the value of the multiplier?

A more detailed consideration of tax changes is given below.

The effect of an increase in income tax rates

If income tax rates are changed there will be a variety of effects on an economy. Given the increase in fiscal deficits and national debts of many countries, it seems likely that taxes will be raised. For example, in the UK, there has been an extra tax band of 50% from April 2010. Higher income tax rates could have the following effects:

- **On income distribution:** the tax system is more **progressive**, making income distribution more equitable.
- **On incentives to work:** an increase in tax rates might have significant disincentive effects. For example, if the basic rate of income tax were raised, there would be less incentive for the unemployed or those not currently participating in the workforce to accept jobs. Similarly, if the higher rate of tax was increased, then people may be less willing to do overtime and more inclined to reduce their working hours, retire early or be less willing to seek promotion.
- **On tax revenues:** some economists consider that, if tax rates are increased too much, tax revenues may actually fall because the disincentives to work are so great. If the higher rate of income tax is increased, then there is likely to be an increase in tax avoidance (legal); tax evasion (illegal); and a rise in the number of tax exiles. The **Laffer curve** illustrated in Figure 6 shows that, if the marginal tax rate is T then tax revenues will be maximised. However, an increase in the marginal tax rate to V will result in a reduction in tax revenues from R to S.

Knowledge check 7

How does an increase in income tax affect the opportunity cost of leisure?

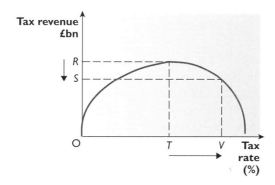

Figure 6 The Laffer curve

- **On the level of economic activity:** an increase in income tax rates would cause a fall in disposable income. In turn, this would cause a reduction in consumption and, therefore, a fall in aggregate demand. It may also be argued that the disincentive effects of higher income tax would cause a leftward shift in the aggregate-supply curve.

Examiner tip

Include an aggregate demand/aggregate supply diagram when considering the implications of changes in income tax.

The effect of an increase in indirect taxes

It is also possible that governments will try to reduce their fiscal deficits by raising indirect taxes. An increase in VAT, for example, could have the following effects:

- **On income distribution:** research suggests that the impact of VAT is broadly **regressive,** so an increase in VAT would cause income distribution to become less even.
- **On incentives to work:** indirect taxes have a less obvious impact on incentives to work than direct taxes. However, it is possible that an increase in direct taxes would encourage people to work harder so that they can maintain their standard of living.

- **On tax revenues:** raising indirect taxes would increase the tax revenues to the government as long as demand for the products and services affected is **price inelastic**.
- **On the rate of inflation:** an increase in VAT will raise the price of most goods and services. If workers and trade unions respond by demanding wage increases to compensate for price rises, then an inflationary wage–price spiral could result.
- **On the level of economic activity:** a rise in VAT would act as a leakage from the circular flow of income. The real incomes of consumers would fall, so causing a fall in aggregate demand. From the perspective of businesses, costs would rise, so causing a fall in aggregate supply.

Public sector borrowing and debt

Public sector net borrowing or fiscal (budget) deficit

Public sector net borrowing (PSNB) is the difference between public expenditure (both current and capital) and tax revenue.

The PSNB is significant for the following reasons.
- Excessive borrowing could be inflationary because aggregate demand would be increasing.
- Public sector net debt (PSNB) must not exceed 3% of GDP to meet the criteria for entry into the euro.
- Taxes as a percentage of GDP give an indication of the size of the state sector relative to the whole economy. This might have significance for foreign direct investment (FDI), since high taxes might act as a deterrent.
- Until 2009, borrowing could only be for capital expenditure over the course of the business cycle to meet the requirements of the Golden Rule (now abandoned).

Public sector net debt or national debt

Public sector net debt (PSND), formerly known as the national debt, is the cumulative total of past government borrowing.
- To meet the sustainable investment rule, this should not exceed 40% of GDP and to meet the conditions for entry into the euro, it should not exceed 60% of GDP.
- As with the PSNB, the absolute size of the PSND is less significant than its size relative to GDP, because this provides an indication of how easily it can be serviced.
- Until 2007, the PSND was below 40% of GDP but the global financial crisis is having a dramatic effect. In 2008, it rose to 47% of GDP and it is expected to reach at least 79% of GDP by 2014. Although this is a signification jump, it is still well below that of some other countries. For example, in 2010, the PSND in Italy was 120% of GDP.

Do large national debts matter?

Some argue that, if the money is being used to finance improvements in infrastructure and other capital projects, then a large PSND might be justified because it would be increasing a country's future productive potential, so making it easier to repay in the future. However, certain problems may arise:

Knowledge check 8

What is the difference between a fiscal deficit and the National Debt?

Edexcel A2 Economics

- There is an **opportunity cost** for future generations: interest payments on the national debt mean that less money will be available for public services.
- **Crowding out:** if the increasing size of the national debt is an indication of an increase in the size of the public sector, then resource or financial crowding out could occur.
- **Danger of inflation:** if the rising national debt has been caused by successive fiscal deficits, then there is a danger that inflationary pressures will develop, since injections will be rising relative to leakages.

In the long run, future governments might be forced to raise taxes and/or cut public expenditure so that the national debt can be reduced.

Examiner tip
Be sure that you can assess the effects of an increase in the size of the National Debt of a country.

Summary

- Public expenditure refers to expenditure by the state.
- There are three distinct categories of public expenditure: current or day-to-day expenditure; capital or long-term expenditure on investment projects; transfer payments that are transfers of money from the state to individuals.
- The size and pattern of public expenditure is determined by a variety of factors, including age and size of the population; GDP and political priorities.

- Taxes may be progressive, proportional or regressive in their impact on income distribution.
- Taxes are divided into direct taxes (those on income and wealth) and indirect taxes (those on expenditure).
- A fiscal or budget deficit occurs when public expenditure exceeds tax revenues, whereas the National Debt is the cumulative total of all past government borrowing.

Examination skills and concepts

- Ability to apply synoptic concepts when considering the objectives of public expenditure and the use of taxes.
- Ability to distinguish between the different sorts of taxes and their effects.
- Ability to analyse the effects of a change in public expenditure or taxation.
- Ability to understand the difference between a fiscal deficit and the public sector net debt.
- Ability to evaluate the causes and consequences of fiscal imbalances.

Common examination errors

- Weak definitions (e.g. stating that progressive taxes imply that the more you earn, the more you pay). This is imprecise, because it could be true of progressive, proportional and regressive taxes.
- Confusion over the meaning of public expenditure, (i.e. it is expenditure by the government *not* expenditure by the public, i.e. consumers).
- Confusing a fiscal deficit with a balance of payments deficit on current account.
- Not addressing the question set (e.g. in questions demanding an analysis of an increase in public expenditure, it would be incorrect to focus the answer on the effects of tax increases to fund the extra public expenditure).

Linkages and common themes

There is plenty of opportunity to include synoptic concepts in this section. The following are some examples:

- Discussion of **price elasticity of demand** (see Unit 1) when considering the impact of an increase in indirect taxes or subsidies.
- As an objective of macroeconomic policy.
- Consideration of **opportunity cost** (see Unit 1) when discussing public expenditure.
- Link with fiscal policy (see Unit 2).

Globalisation
The meaning of globalisation

There is no precise definition of the term 'globalisation' and it is used to refer to a variety of ways in which countries are becoming more and more closely integrated, not just in the economic sense, but also culturally and politically.

However, one of the best definitions of globalisation in the economic sense is by Peter Jay, who was the BBC's economics correspondent in 1996: 'The ability to produce any good or service anywhere in the world, using raw materials, components, capital and technology from anywhere, sell the resulting output anywhere and place the profits anywhere.'

It should be understood that globalisation is not a new phenomenon because there have been many periods in history when there was considerable integration between countries; for example, during the height of Roman empire. However, the pace of global integration has increased considerably over the last 30 years.

Characteristics of globalisation

Globalisation, in the economic sense, is characterised by the following:

- an increase in trade as a proportion of world GDP
- increased movements of financial capital between countries
- increased international specialisation and division of labour. It is increasingly common for parts and components of products to be made in different countries and for assembly to occur in another country.
- the growing importance of transnational companies (TNCs) and foreign direct investment

Factors contributing to globalisation

A variety of factors have contributed to the increased economic integration of countries.

One of the most significant is the **fall in transport costs**. In real terms the price of transporting goods has decreased significantly, enabling goods to be imported and exported more cheaply. Coupled with this has been a **decline in the cost of communications**. In particular, the cost of using the internet has fallen greatly over the last 20 years and its availability has increased.

The **lowering of trade barriers** since the Second World War has been a major factor in the growth of world trade. The World Trade Organization (WTO) — formerly the General Agreement on Tariffs and Trade — has been responsible for negotiating reductions in tariffs and other barriers to trade in rounds of talks, the most recent of which is the Doha Round.

Both the **collapse of communism** and the **opening up of China** to world trade have contributed to globalisation. Countries which were previously not open to foreign direct investment (FDI) became much more integrated into the world trading system. **Transnational (multinational) companies** have taken advantage of the reduction in trade barriers and the development of the internet to organise trade on a global scale.

Knowledge check 9

How might a significant increase in transport costs affect globalisation?

Benefits and disadvantages of globalisation

Benefits

Free trade enables the application of the **law of comparative advantage** (see pages 22–23), which suggests that, when countries specialise in the goods in which they have a comparative advantage (i.e. the goods can be produced at a lower opportunity cost) then world output and living standards will increase. It is evident that the growth of world trade in both goods and services has been associated with increased growth in real GDP.

- For consumers, globalisation may mean a wider choice of goods at a lower price.
- For producers, there are likely to be benefits in terms of lower production costs as a result of offshoring and also economies of scale.

Disadvantages and problems

Globalisation has been criticised on the basis that it has **promoted exploitation** of workers, children, farmers and the environment. Similarly, health and safety laws and regulations are usually less demanding in developing countries.

The **external costs** associated with trade are becoming increasingly apparent, especially in relation to environmental degradation which results in global warming. Consumers are becoming more aware of 'food miles' (i.e. how many miles food has travelled to reach the consumer). It may be argued, therefore, that increased trade is not sustainable in terms of the environment.

Globalisation has also been associated with **increased inequality.** For example, rich countries have much greater access to the internet than poor countries. Given that much wealth creation is dependent on the ready availability of information, the poorest developing countries are at a severe disadvantage.

Some argue that the liberalisation of financial markets has been associated with **increased global instability**, as evidenced by the financial crises in Asia at the end of the 1990s and, more recently, the **global credit crunch** following the collapse in confidence of the banking system. It is also argued that the **global imbalances**

Knowledge check 10

What is the link between savings ratios and global imbalances?

Examiner tip

The arguments for and against globalisation overlap with many other areas of this unit, so it is useful to revisit these once you have understood those topics.

currently experienced (for example, the deficits on the current account of the balance of payments in USA and surpluses in China) are unsustainable.

The global financial crisis that became particularly evident in 2008 has led to a development sometimes described as **deglobalisation,** in which countries adopt protectionist policies in an attempt to protect domestic employment. Obviously, this leads to a decline in specialisation and trade. Examples of protectionism in 2009 include the subsidies given to the car industry in the USA; the increased tariffs imposed on imported cars by Russia and the EU raising duties on imported Vietnamese shoes.

International trade

Globalisation has led to a phenomenal increase in world trade. One measure is to consider exports as a proportion of world GDP. Figure 7 shows that world trade has grown in most years since 1970 and by an average of at least 6% per annum. The dramatic fall in world trade at the end of 2008 and in 2009 may be regarded as a temporary reversal in the process of globalisation (or deglobalisation).

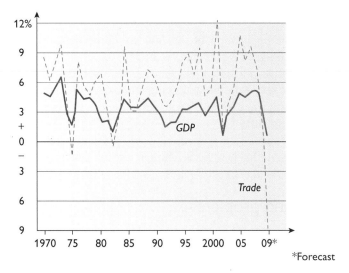

Figure 7 World trade and GDP: percentage change on previous year

Source: *The Economist*, 26 March 2009

The pattern of world trade has also been greatly affected by the entry of China as a major manufacturer. For example, Figure 8 shows the growth of China's share of world exports as a proportion of total exports relative to other major exporters.

The basis of free trade: the law of comparative advantage

This law states that, even if one country has an **absolute advantage** in the production of all goods, it can still benefit from specialisation and trade if it specialises in the production of goods in which it has a **comparative advantage** (i.e. if it specialises in the production of those products in which its opportunity cost is lowest). The crucial

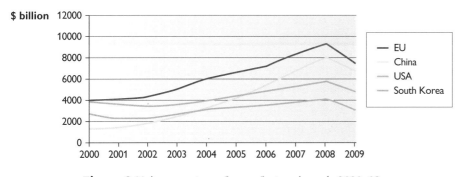

Figure 8 Major exporters of manufactured goods 2000–09

Source: International Trade Statistics, 2010 (www.wto.org)

requirement is that there must be a difference in the opportunity cost of producing the products. The following example illustrates this principle.

Suppose countries A and B both produce two products — palm oil and televisions. They can both produce the following amounts of these products with the same quantity of resources:

Country	Palm oil	Televisions
A	20,000	10,000
B	8,000	8,000

Clearly, country A has an absolute advantage in the production of both palm oil and televisions. If each country devotes half its resources to the production of each product, then output would be as follows:

Country	Palm oil	Televisions
A	10,000	5,000
B	4,000	4,000
Total	14,000	9,000

To determine whether trade will be worthwhile, the **opportunity costs** must be calculated:

	Opportunity cost of producing 1 kilo of palm oil	Opportunity cost of producing 1 television
A	½	2
B	1	1

From the table, it can be seen that country A has a comparative advantage in palm oil (because the opportunity cost is lower), while country B has a comparative advantage in televisions.

For trade to be beneficial, the terms of trade must lie between the opportunity cost ratios. In this case, the terms of trade must lie between 1 kilo of palm oil and 2 kilos of palm oil for 1 television.

The terms of trade are measured as follows:

$$\frac{\text{Index of export prices}}{\text{Index of import prices}} \times 100$$

You should note that, if the opportunity costs were the same, then there would be no benefit from specialisation and trade.

However, despite widespread acceptance of the law of comparative advantage among economists and the benefits of free trade, various criticisms can be made:

- Free trade is not necessarily fair trade (i.e. the rich countries might exert their **monopsony** power to force producers in developing countries to accept low prices).
- The law of comparative advantage is based on unrealistic assumptions such as constant costs of production, zero transport costs and no barriers to trade.

Limits to free trade: the case for protectionism

The term 'protectionism' refers to measures designed to limit free trade. Arguments supporting the need for protectionism include the following:

- To **protect infant industries:** this argument might be particularly relevant to developing countries that are in the process of industrialisation. Without protection, infant industries might be unable to compete because they have yet to establish themselves and are too small to benefit from economies of scale.
- To **protect geriatric industries:** these are industries that might demand protection so that they have time to restructure and rationalise production so that they can become competitive once again. Typically, these occur in developed economies that are losing their comparative advantage.
- To **ensure employment protection:** cheap imports might threaten jobs in the domestic economy and workers might demand that the government takes action to limit imports.
- To **prevent dumping:** the term dumping refers to goods exported to another country at below the average cost of production. It is a form of predatory pricing and, if it can be proved, is illegal under World Trade Organization (WTO) rules. This is one of the few arguments in favour of protectionism that can be justified in terms of economic theory because it unfairly distorts comparative advantage.
- To **correct a balance of payments deficit on current account:** restrictions on imports might help to reduce the imbalance between the value of imports and the value of exports. However, under a system of floating exchange rates, it is possible that this correction will happen automatically.
- To **restrict imports from countries whose health and safety regulations and environmental regulations are less stringent:** some argue that developing countries might have an unfair competitive advantage because production is not subject to the same laws and regulations that apply to developed countries, so enabling them to produce at a lower average cost.
- For **strategic reasons:** a country might introduce protectionist policies on goods of strategic importance in time of war so that it is not dependent on imports. Food, defence equipment and energy are items frequently used as examples of such goods.

- To **raise tax revenue:** tariffs might be an important source of tax revenue for developing countries.
- **In retaliation:** barriers to trade might be imposed by a country because another country has restricted the import of its goods.

Types of protection/import barriers

There are numerous ways by which free trade can be prevented. The most common are **tariffs, quotas, subsidies to domestic producers** and **administrative regulations**. In countries where the exchange rate is not freely floating, the authorities might also hold down the value of the currency artificially to give their goods a competitive advantage (China has been accused of adopting such a policy in recent years).

These are sometimes referred to as customs duties: they are simply taxes on imported goods. Figure 9 illustrates the effect of a tariff.

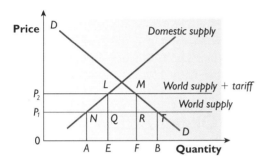

Figure 9 The effects of imposing a tariff

Examiner tip

Knowledge of the tariff diagram is very useful in explaining a range of possible effects.

Before the tariff is imposed

- the price paid by consumers is *OP1*; domestic output is *OA*; imports are *AB*

Once the tariff is imposed

- the price paid by consumers rises to *P2*, so reducing consumers' surplus by *P1P2MT*
- domestic output rises to *OE*, so increasing producer surplus by *P1P2LN*
- imports fall to *EF*
- tax revenue to the government is *QLMR*
- net welfare loss areas are *NLQ* and *RMT*

Knowledge check 12

What determines the impact of a tariff on imports?

Quotas

Import quotas place a physical restriction on the amount of goods that can be imported. They have similar effects to those of tariffs, in that the price of imported goods will rise and domestic producers should gain more business. However, unlike tariffs, the government does not receive any revenue.

Subsidies to domestic producers

Grants given to domestic producers artificially lower their production costs, so enabling their goods to be more competitive. Subsidies therefore act as a barrier to trade.

Administrative regulations

These take a variety of forms, including labelling, health and safety regulations, environmental standards and documentation on country of origin. In effect, such regulations increase the costs of foreign producers and so act as a barrier to trade.

The case against protectionism

There are several problems with protectionism including:
- inefficient resource allocation: trade barriers distort comparative advantage and reduce specialisation, which will result in lower world output and, therefore, lower living standards
- higher prices and less choice for consumers
- less incentive for domestic producers to become more efficient
- difficulty of removing trade barriers. Once such barriers are introduced, it might prove to be difficult to remove them because of the adverse effect on domestic producers.

The World Trade Organization

The primary aim of the World Trade Organization (WTO) is to **liberalise trade,** i.e. to lower trade barriers. It does this by providing governments with a forum for negotiating trade agreements. Since the creation of the General Agreement on Tariffs and Trade (GATT), which was the forerunner of the WTO, there have been eight rounds of talks, with the ninth round — the Doha Development Agenda — still being negotiated (since 2001).

In addition to promoting free trade, the WTO performs other functions including:
- the settlement of disputes between member countries
- the provision of a system of trade rules

Underlying WTO agreements are a set of principles that include:
- **Most-favoured-nation principle:** which implies that countries cannot discriminate between their trading partners. For example, a reduction in a tariff for one country must be extended to all countries.
- **National treatment:** imported and locally produced products must be treated equally once the foreign goods have entered the market.

> **Examiner tip**
> The role of the WTO in reducing trade barriers may be linked to the law of comparative advantage.

While the WTO has been successful in bringing about substantial reductions in tariffs on manufactured goods, e.g. industrialised countries' tariffs on industrial goods averaged just 4% by the mid-1990s, it has been less successful in reducing barriers to the trade in services. Further, there has been a growth in the use of non-tariff barriers, especially administrative regulations, which has, to some extent, offset the gains from the reduction in tariffs.

Trading blocs

Regional trade blocs are intergovernmental associations that manage and promote trade activities for specific regions of the world. Trading blocs may take several forms:

- **Free trade areas**. Trade barriers are removed between member countries, but individual members can still impose tariffs and quotas on countries outside the area. An example is the North Atlantic Free Trade Area (NAFTA).
- **Customs unions**. The characteristics of customs unions include free trade between member states and a **common external tariff** on goods imported from outside the bloc. An example is the European Union.
- **Common markets**. These are customs unions but with the added dimension that it is not only goods and services that can be moved freely within the area (between member states), but also factors of production (especially labour).
- **Monetary unions**. These are customs unions that adopt a **common currency**. The euro zone area of the EU is an example of such a union.

Examiner tip
Trading blocs are *not* blocks on trade such as tariffs; they are groups of countries that agree to trade freely between themselves.

Trading blocs and the WTO

The existence of trading blocs has two significant consequences:
- trade creation
- trade diversion

Trade creation occurs because the removal of trade barriers results in increased specialisation and trade according to the law of comparative advantage.

Trade diversion occurs because member countries may now buy goods from other member countries (which are not subject to tariffs) rather than from countries outside the bloc (which are subject to tariffs). Therefore, there is a diversion of trade from lower-cost countries outside the bloc to higher-cost countries inside the union. Consequently, trade diversion results in an inefficient allocation of resources.

Nevertheless, it may be argued that the growth in both the number and size of trading blocs has contributed to the WTO goal of promoting free trade.

Knowledge check 13
What is the key feature of any trading bloc?

Summary

- Globalisation refers to the increased economic integration between countries through, for example, increased trade.
- Many factors have contributed to increased globalisation, including: the lowering of trade barriers; lower communication and transport costs; the opening up of China.
- Benefits of globalisation may be analysed using the law of comparative advantage and costs, using concepts such as external costs and increased inequality.
- The law of comparative advantage states that trade between two nations can be beneficial to both if each specialises in the production of a good with lower opportunity cost.
- Arguments for protectionism include: employment protection; prevention of dumping; protection of infant industries; retaliation.
- Protectionism may take several forms, such as tariffs, quotas, subsidies to domestic producers, and non-tariff barriers.
- The main roles of the WTO are to promote free trade and settle trade disputes.
- Trading blocs are groups of countries that trade freely among themselves but set trade barriers against non-members.

Examination skills and concepts
- Understanding of the growing interdependence between economies.
- Ability to differentiate between the costs and benefits of globalisation.
- Ability to explain the basis of free trade in terms of the law of comparative advantage.
- Ability to use the tariff diagram to illustrate the implications of tariffs, including welfare losses.
- Evaluation of the possible conflicts between trading blocs and the WTO.

Common examination errors
- Imprecise diagrammatic analysis, especially in the case of tariffs.
- Misinterpreting trading blocs as protectionist measures.

Linkages and common themes
- Application of opportunity cost to the law of comparative advantage.
- Supply and demand analysis in considering tariffs and quotas (see Unit 1).

The balance of payments and exchange rates

The components of the balance of payments

The balance of payments is a record of all financial transactions between one country and other countries. When there is an inflow of foreign currency into the UK, this is recorded as a positive item, whereas when there is an outflow of foreign currency, this is recorded as a negative item.

The main components of the balance of payments are the **current account** and the **capital and financial account** (formerly called the capital account).

The current account

This is composed of the following:
- The **trade in goods balance:** this is the value of goods exported minus the value of goods imported.
- The **trade in services balance:** this is the value of services exported minus the value of services imported.
- The **income balance:** this is income flows into the country from non-residents minus income flows out of the country from residents to non-residents, e.g. income refers to compensation to employees and investment income.
- **Current transfers:** relates to items such as food aid and the UK's contribution to the EU's Common Agricultural Policy.

The capital and financial account

This comprises transactions associated with changes of ownership of the UK's foreign financial assets and liabilities. A key factor influencing the financial account is **foreign direct investment (FDI)**. Also included are portfolio investment in shares and bonds, changes in foreign exchange reserves and the short-term capital flows, often referred to as 'hot money' flows, associated with speculation.

The balance on this account should exactly offset the current account balance (although, in practice, there is a significant component comprising errors and omissions).

Current account deficits and surpluses

For many years, the UK has had a deficit on the current account. In particular, the trade in goods balance has deteriorated over a number of years, as shown in Figure 10.

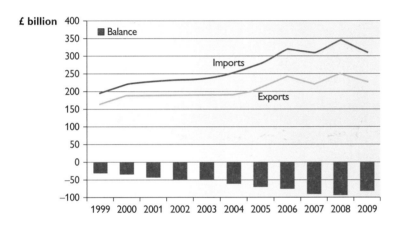

Figure 10 The UK trade in goods balance

Source: www.ons.gov.uk

The main reasons for the UK's deficit on its trade in goods balance include:
- the high value of sterling 1996–2008
- continuous economic growth 1992–2008 — the UK has a high marginal propensity to import and so rising real incomes have led to a significant increase in imports
- relatively low productivity of the UK's workers resulting in higher average costs
- the relocation of manufacturing to countries with lower labour costs (e.g. China and Eastern European countries)
- the 'Chindia effect': the industrialisation of China and India has led to a flood of cheap imports into the UK

Surpluses on the trade in services have been insufficient to offset the deficits on the trade in goods balance.

The implications of global imbalances

Like the UK, the USA has experienced large current account deficits, while in contrast, China has experienced huge current account surpluses. Whether such

Knowledge check 14

What factors might cause a balance of trade surplus?

global imbalances can be sustained in the long run is a major question. On the one hand, if the deficits are easily financed by inflows on the financial account, there may be no cause for concern. Further, under a system of floating exchange rates over time, there should be an automatic adjustment (i.e. deficit would cause the exchange rate to fall). On the other hand, continuous deficits by the USA have, in effect, been financed by the Chinese, which may not be a sustainable option in the long run. Further, exchange rate adjustments might occur suddenly, as when the value of the pound fell by 27% between July 2008 and March 2009.

Exchange rates

The exchange rate is the rate at which one currency exchanges for another; in other words it is the *price* of one currency in terms of another, e.g. £1 = $1.50.

Causes of changes in the exchange rate

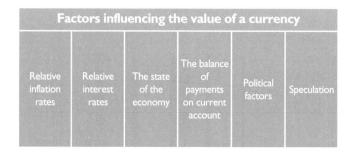

Figure 11 Factors influencing exchange rates

As Figure 11 shows, a variety of factors can influence the value of a country's currency (under a system of floating exchange rates), including the following:

- **Relative inflation rates:** if the country's inflation rate is higher than that of its major competitors then, according to **purchasing power parity (PPP) analysis**, it would be expected that the value of the currency would fall. The PPP rate is the rate at which a particular product would be sold at the same price in the UK and abroad when expressed in a common currency.
- **Relative interest rates:** if the UK has higher interest rates than those of other countries, then foreigners with surplus balances are likely to place them in UK banks, so increasing the demand for sterling and causing the value of the pound to increase.
- **The state of the economy:** for example, if the UK economy is performing well, then this will increase the confidence of speculators and foreign investors, who will buy sterling, so causing its value to rise.
- **The balance of payments on current account:** if there is a persistent deficit on the current account, then the supply of the currency would be high relative to demand for it and the value of the currency would be expected to fall. In practice, this factor is not significant because the flows of money associated with trade are small compared with 'hot money' flows and other transactions recorded in the financial account.
- **Political stability:** in developing countries, instability may cause a loss of **confidence in the country's currency**.

- **Speculation:** the exchange rate might be affected by speculation concerning a range of possible events, including factors such as the future state of the economy, a change in government or impending strikes. For example, if it is expected that the economy will recover from a recession much more quickly than originally thought then speculators may buy sterling, so pushing up its value.

Effects of a change in the exchange rate of a currency

Suppose that the value of the pound against the dollar falls, e.g. from £1 = $2.00 to £1 = $1.50. There are two effects.

- It will make the price of goods exported from the UK **decrease** in the country of sale (e.g. a bottle of UK whisky costing £20 would have sold for $40 in the USA but will now sell for $30).
- It will make the price of goods imported into the UK **increase** (e.g. a $10 bottle of Californian wine would have been priced at £5 in UK but will now cost £6.67).

Therefore, a fall in the value of the pound makes UK goods more competitive. The consequence of this is that demand for exports is likely to rise while the demand for imports is likely to fall. This is likely to cause a reduction in the size of the deficit on the current account of the balance of payments.

The Marshall–Lerner condition

For there to be an improvement in the current account, the Marshall–Lerner condition must be fulfilled (i.e. the sum of the price elasticities of demand for imports and exports must be greater than 1).

The J-curve effect

It is possible that there could be a time lag before the full effects of the depreciation of the currency work through the economy, such that in the short run, the sum of the price elasticities of demand would be less than 1 but greater than 1 in the long run. This gives rise to the **J-curve effect,** as illustrated in Figure 12.

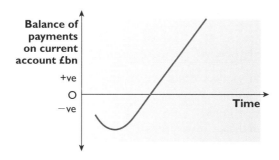

Figure 12 The J-curve effect

Initially, the current account deteriorates, since demand for imports is price inelastic because of contracts or stocks of goods. Also, demand for exports may be inelastic because it takes time for consumers to adjust to the price changes. In the longer term, demand for both imports and exports may become more elastic and, if the Marshall–Lerner condition is fulfilled, the current account will improve.

Knowledge check 15

What is likely to happen to the value of the euro if members of the eurozone default on their debts?

Examiner tip

Remember that a fall in the value of a country's currency causes an increase in the price competitiveness of its goods and services, whereas a rise causes a decrease in the price competitiveness of its goods and services.

Knowledge check 16

What would be the effect on the current account of the balance of payments following a depreciation in the value of the currency if the sum of PEDs for exports and imports is less than between 0 and −1?

European Monetary Union (EMU)

The euro was launched on 1 January 1999. Initially, there were 11 members of the euro zone; a further five countries had joined by 2009. Denmark and the UK agreed an opt-out clause, while many of the newer members, together with Sweden, have yet to meet the convergence criteria.

These convergence criteria are set out below:
- The fiscal deficit has to be below 3% of gross domestic product (GDP).
- The public sector net debt (national debt) has to be less than 60% of GDP.
- Countries should have an inflation rate within 1.5% of the three EU countries with the lowest rate.
- Long-term interest rates must be within 2% of the three lowest interest rates in the EU.
- Exchange rates must be kept within 'normal' fluctuation margins of Europe's exchange-rate mechanism.

In addition to the convergence criteria, the chancellor set out five tests to determine whether or not the UK should join the euro, to which others were added in 2002:
- Are the business cycles of the UK and European economies converging, so that interest rates set by the European Central Bank will be suited to the needs of the UK economy?
- Are the economies flexible enough to cope if there are external shocks to the world economy?
- Will joining the euro encourage foreign direct investment into the UK?
- Will joining the euro be good for financial services?
- Will joining the euro promote higher economic growth, stability and a long-term increase in employment?

Further tests were added in 2002, the most important of which was the sterling–euro exchange rate. Clearly, the government would not wish to join the euro if it believed that the pound was over-valued against the euro.

Arguments about the costs and benefits of membership of the euro have continued since its inception.

The main advantages of monetary union

- Elimination of transaction costs, i.e. commission charged on exchange of currencies. However, these represent only a small proportion of GDP.
- Price transparency: it is easy to compare prices of goods across the countries which have adopted the euro. Competition within the euro zone should, therefore, increase and the likelihood of price discrimination should be diminished. However, there is still evidence of price differences between members of the euro zone.
- Easier trading conditions for firms inside the euro zone, which might enable them to benefit from further economies of scale.
- Encouragement to transnational companies to invest in euro zone countries as opposed to the countries of non-members. However, the evidence that this has happened is weak.

The main disadvantages of monetary union

- Loss of independent monetary policy, i.e. countries no longer have the ability to set their own interest rates. The interest rate is set by the European Central Bank (ECB). However, this means that the needs of individual countries are placed second to those of the euro zone members as a whole.
- The ECB's inflation target is to keep inflation below 2%, which is a more stringent target than that of the Bank of England. A criticism is that this policy is less flexible and more deflationary than that of the UK.
- Loss of exchange rate flexibility against other countries which have adopted the euro.
- Transition costs (i.e. cost of changing slot machines, menus, price lists and so on, to the new currency).
- Meeting the requirements of the growth and stability pact might result in a slower rate of economic growth which could, in turn, result in a higher level of unemployment. For example, countries are not supposed to run fiscal deficits higher than 3% of their GDP. In practice, this rule has not been adhered to by some countries and the recent global financial crisis has led to calls for it to be relaxed.

Examiner tip

Consider the advantages and disadvantages of monetary union in the light of the sovereign debt crisis starting in 2010.

Summary

- The current account of the balance of payments is mainly concerned with the trade in goods and services between countries.
- The financial account is important when considering FDI and 'hot money flows' between countries.
- Current account deficits may be caused by factors including: a lack of competitiveness; an overvalued exchange rate; relatively low productivity; and non-price factors such as poor quality and design.
- Global imbalances arise when some countries have persistent current account deficits while others have persistent current account surpluses.
- In a free market, exchange rates are determined by the supply of and demand for currencies on the foreign exchange market.

- An exchange rate may be affected by factors such as confidence; relative interest rates; relative inflation rates; expectations about the future state of the economy.
- A depreciation in the value of a country's currency may increase the competitiveness of a country's goods and services but the impact on the current account of the balance of payments will depend on the Marshall-Lerner condition.
- Monetary union occurs when countries give up their own currencies and adopt a single currency. The key advantages are absence of transactions costs; price transparency; greater certainty for producers within the union while the key disadvantages are loss of independent monetary policy and loss of exchange rate flexibility.

Examination skills and concepts

- Understanding the main components of the balance of payments accounts and being able to assess the impact on these components of changes in external factors (e.g. an increase in foreign direct investment).
- Ability to analyse the effect of changes in the exchange rate on other macroeconomic variables.
- Assessing the case for and against membership of the euro zone.

Common examination errors

- Confusion between a balance of payments deficit and a fiscal deficit.
- Confusion over the difference between components of the current account and components of the financial account.
- A lack of clarity in explaining the effects of a change in the exchange rate on international trade.
- Assuming that countries and groups such as the USA, EU and UK can 'devalue' or 'revalue' their currencies.

Linkages and common themes

- The balance of payments accounts (see Unit 2).
- Causes of changes in exchange rates under a system of floating exchange rates: application of supply and demand analysis (see Unit 1).
- Price elasticities of demand for import and exports (see Unit 1) when considering exchange rate changes.

International competitiveness

A country's 'international competitiveness' refers to its ability to sell its goods and services in domestic and international markets at a price and quality that is attractive in those markets. Competitiveness may be measured in terms of **price** or **non-price factors**. The non-price factors include quality, design, reliability and availability.

Measures of international competitiveness

These measures include:

- **relative unit labour costs**: the measurement of labour costs in one country relative to those in another country. To make international comparisons, the figures are converted into a single currency and expressed as an index number.
- **relative productivity measures**: e.g. output per worker per hour worked
- **composite indices**: such as the **global competitiveness index** produced by the World Economic Forum. This is based on 12 pillars of competitiveness, as follows:
  - institutions
  - infrastructure
  - macroeconomic stability
  - health and primary education
  - higher education and training
  - goods market efficiency
  - labour market efficiency
  - financial market sophistication
  - technological readiness
  - market size
  - business sophistication
  - innovation

The top 15 rankings for 2011–12 are:

1 Switzerland
2 Singapore
3 Sweden
4 Finland
5 USA

6 Germany
7 Netherlands
8 Denmark
9 Japan
10 UK

11 Hong Kong SAR
12 Canada
13 Taiwan

14 Qatar
15 Belgium

Factors influencing international competitiveness

Real exchange rate

Competitiveness is determined by a variety of factors but one of the most important is a country's real exchange rate, which is the nominal exchange rate adjusted for changes in price levels between economies.

More precisely:

$$\text{real exchange rate} = \frac{\text{nominal exchange rate} \times \text{domestic price level}}{\text{foreign price level}}$$

There will be a depreciation in the real exchange rate if the nominal exchange rate falls or if the prices of goods abroad rise relative to prices in this country. Therefore, a fall in the real exchange rate will cause an increase in the competitiveness of a country's goods.

In contrast, the real exchange rate will increase if the nominal exchange rate rises or if the UK price level rises relative to the foreign price level. Consequently, an appreciation of the real exchange rate is associated with a fall in the country's competitiveness.

Wage costs and non-wage costs

Wage costs are the most important cost of production for many industries. Consequently, if wages are higher in the UK than in China, it is likely that the prices of the goods in the UK will be higher than those of China if productivity is ignored.

Non-wage costs are also significant for international competitiveness. These include:
- national insurance contributions paid by employers (taxes on employment)
- health and safety regulations
- environmental regulations
- employment protection and anti-discrimination laws
- contributions into company pension schemes

These non-wage costs are frequently much higher in developed countries than in developing countries and so have the effect of reducing the international competitiveness of goods and services from developed countries.

Other factors

- **labour productivity:** usually defined as the output per worker per hour worked. In turn this is influenced by:
- **education and training:** which influences the level of:
- **human capital:** defined as the knowledge and skills of the workforce and by:

- the amount and quality of **capital equipment** per worker
- **research and development:** in turn, this might lead to technological advances which may have dramatic effects on productivity and competitiveness
- **infrastructure:** of the country (e.g. roads, railways, telecommunications, power generating stations and water supply)
- **labour market flexibility:** this is affected by factors such as the ease of hiring and firing workers, willingness of workers to work part-time or on flexible contracts and the strength of trade unions

Measures and policies to increase competitiveness

Firms can improve the competitiveness of their products by investing in new capital equipment with the aim of raising productivity. They could improve the design and quality of their products through research and development.

Governments can try to improve international competitiveness through a variety of **supply-side policies** (see pages 12–13). Of particular relevance are the following:
- measures to increase the occupational mobility such as education and training schemes
- macroeconomic stability, e.g. a low and stable inflation rate; sound public finances; a relatively stable exchange rate; steady economic growth
- public sector reform aimed at reducing red tape
- government expenditure to improve infrastructure
- privatisation
- incentives for investment such as tax breaks if companies use profits for investment rather than for distribution to shareholders

You should note that international agreements are likely to prevent individual countries increasing their competitiveness by raising tariffs. For example, the UK cannot simply introduce tariffs on goods from other EU countries because of its legal obligations as a member of the EU. Similarly, most countries are members of the World Trade Organization (WTO), whose rules prevent a country unilaterally imposing protectionist measures unless there is justifiable case.

Further, it is not correct to suggest that 'the UK government could devalue its currency' because the pound is a floating currency. Also, since the Bank of England is independent, the government cannot directly engineer a depreciation in the exchange rate of the pound through a reduction in interest rates because control over interest rates is no longer in its hands.

The significance of international competitiveness

A fall in international competitiveness is likely to be reflected in a deterioration in the trade in goods balance of the balance of payments. In turn, this could result in an increase in unemployment, especially in industries in which exports are significant. A fall in exports could have a negative multiplier effect on GDP, so causing a reduction in economic growth.

Summary

- International competitiveness reflects the ability of a country to sell its goods and services in world markets.
- The key factors influencing competitiveness are relative unit labour costs; relative productivity rates; education and training; capital per worker; infrastructure; non-wage factors including

National Insurance contributions; regulations, e.g. relating to the environment, and to health and safety.

- International competitiveness could be increased by supply-side policies or by a depreciation of the country's currency.

Examination skills and concepts

- Understanding different measures of competitiveness.
- Understanding the real exchange rate.
- Ability to evaluate the significance of competitiveness for an economy.
- Ability to evaluate different measures to increase competitiveness.

Common examination errors

- Confusion between production and productivity.
- Confusion between the nominal and real exchange rate.

Linkages and common themes

- This section has close links with productivity, supply-side polices and the balance of payments (see Unit 2).
- Obviously, there are links with other parts of this unit, including the exchange rate, globalisation and the factors influencing growth in developing countries.

Poverty and inequality

Measures of poverty

Absolute poverty

According to the World Bank, people are considered to be living in absolute poverty if their incomes fall below the minimum level to meet basic needs such as food, shelter, clothing, access to clean water, sanitation facilities, education and information. This minimum level is usually called the **poverty line**. The World Bank has set international poverty lines at $1 and $2 a day in purchasing power parity terms. In 2008, the lower level was reset at $1.25 at 2005 GDP measured at purchasing power parity.

One of the key Millennium Development Goals is to halve the number of people living in absolute poverty by 2015. Although the poverty line is designed to provide an objective measure of poverty, the World Bank recognises that what constitutes a minimum level of income to meet basic needs is likely to vary over time and between societies.

Relative poverty

People are considered to be in relative poverty if they are living below a certain income threshold in a particular country. It may be measured by calculating the percentage of the population living below 50% of the median income. Therefore, the concept of relative poverty is:

- highly subjective
- subject to change over time
- not comparable between countries (i.e. someone deemed relatively poor in the USA would be regarded as being incredibly rich in Malawi)

Relative poverty arises from inequality (see below).

Composite measures of poverty

A composite measure of poverty, devised by the UN as a measure of deprivation, is provided by the **human poverty index (HPI).** There are in fact two indices, the first of which, **HPI–1**, is a measure of deprivation in the poorest countries of the world. There are three elements in this index:

(1) The percentage of people not expected to reach the age of 40.
(2) The percentage of the population who are illiterate.
(3) The percentage of children who are illiterate and the percentage of the population who do not have access to safe water and healthcare.

To provide a measure more relevant to developed countries, **HPI–2** has been developed. This has the following elements:

(1) Probability at birth of not surviving to age 60 (times 100).
(2) Adults lacking functional literacy skills.
(3) Population below income poverty line (50% of median adjusted household disposable income).
(4) Rate of long-term unemployment (lasting 12 months or more).

Measurements of inequality

Factors influencing inequality

A variety of factors influence the degree of inequality in a country including the following.

- education and training
- wage rate
- inheritance
- ownership of assets, e.g. houses and shares
- pension rights
- unemployment
- social benefits
- the tax system

The Lorenz curve

The degree of inequality can be measured using a Lorenz curve, which plots the cumulative percentage of the population against the cumulative percentage of total income. The 45° line represents perfect equality such that the poorest 10% of the population would receive 10% of the income, the poorest 20% of the population would receive 20% of the income and so on. The curved line represents an unequal distribution of income. The areas *A* and *B* are used in the calculation of the Gini coefficient; see Figure 13.

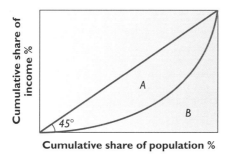

Figure 13 The Lorenz curve

Examiner tip

Make sure that you can draw an accurately labelled Lorenz curve diagram and can show an increase or decrease in inequality.

The Gini coefficient

This is a measure of the degree of inequality in a country. It is calculated as follows:

$$G = \frac{A}{A+B}$$

where A represents the area between the diagonal line and the Lorenz curve and B represents the area under the Lorenz curve. The Gini coefficient will have a value of between 0 and 1, with 0 representing absolute equality (i.e. the Lorenz curve and line of total equality are merged) and 1 absolute inequality (i.e. the Lorenz curve would lie along the horizontal and vertical axes). The Gini coefficient may also be expressed as a percentage:

$$G = \frac{A}{A+B} \times 100$$

Knowledge check 18

What would happen to the Lorenz curve if inequality within a country increased?

Consequences of inequality

Inequality is often regarded as an inevitable cost associated with economic growth. However, it may be argued that inequality itself may be a constraint on growth and development because:

* the very poor will have no collateral and so will be unable to start their own businesses
* absolute poverty could remain high in countries where inequality is high
* those on low incomes will have a low marginal propensity to save, so limiting funds available for investment, while those on high incomes may spend a large amount of their incomes on imported goods or may transfer their incomes to other countries (known as capital flight; see page 43)
* there may be socially undesirable consequences of inequality, such as an increase in the crime rate

Summary

- Absolute poverty refers to people who have insufficient resources to meet their basic needs whereas relative poverty refers to those living below a certain income level.
- Poverty may be measured by composite indices such as HPI–1 or HPI–2.
- Wealth and income inequality may be caused by a variety of factors, including: inheritance; ownership of assets; education; wage rates; age; pension entitlements; unemployment; taxes, and social benefits.
- Inequality may be measured by reference to the Lorenz curve and Gini coefficient.
- Inequality may limit growth and development, e.g. because those in absolute poverty will be unable to obtain loans to start businesses.

Examination skills and concepts

- Understanding the difference between absolute poverty and relative poverty.
- Ability to explain the factors influencing inequality.
- Understanding of the Lorenz curve and Gini coefficient.

Common examination errors

- Confusion between absolute and relative poverty.
- Failing to interpret the Lorenz curve and Gini coefficient correctly.

Linkages and common themes

- Link with measures of development, e.g. the human development index (see Unit 2).
- There are links with the section on public finance (see pages 14–20), in particular, the use of progressive taxation and transfer payments (social benefits) in reducing inequality.

Limits to growth and development

Economic growth is measured in terms of changes in real GDP. However, **economic development** cannot be defined so precisely. It is a multidimensional concept which refers to changes in living standards and welfare over time. Unlike economic growth, therefore, economic development is a **normative** concept dependent on value judgements. In order to provide some measure of development, various composite measures are used. The most common of these is the **human development index (HDI),** which includes GDP per head (measured at purchasing power parity), health (measured in terms of life expectancy at birth) and education (measured in terms of mean years of schooling and expected years of schooling). However, this is a narrow measure of development because it ignores a range of other indicators such as:

- the proportion of the population with access to clean water
- the proportion of the working population employed in agriculture
- energy consumption per person
- proportion of households with internet access
- mobile phones per thousand of population

Examiner tip
Ensure that you can explain the difference between economic growth and economic development.

Constraints on growth and development

While all countries face constraints on their growth and development, there is an enormous difference in the scale of the constraints affecting developed and developing countries. Further, the problems facing any particular developing or developed country vary considerably. It is important, therefore, to have some knowledge of particular countries in order to give relevant examples. This section and the next one focus primarily on problems facing developing countries (see Figure 14).

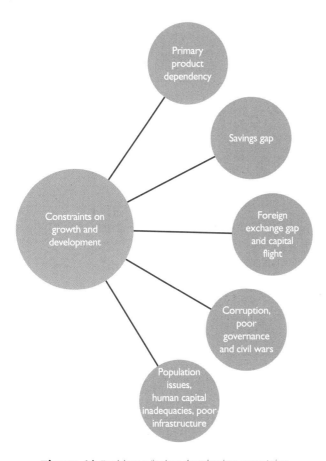

Figure 14 Problems facing developing countries

Primary product dependency

Primary products may be divided into hard commodities, such as copper, tin and iron ore and soft commodities, which include most agricultural crops, such as wheat, palm oil, rice and fruit. A range of issues face countries dependent on primary products, including the following:

- **Price fluctuations:** given their price inelasticity of supply and demand, any demand-side or supply-side shock will result in a significant price change.
- **Fluctuations in producers' incomes and foreign exchange earnings:** since demand is price inelastic, then a fall in price will cause total revenue to fall and, in turn, the foreign currency earnings from exports to fall.
- **Difficulty of planning investment and output:** the price fluctuations cause uncertainty, which is a deterrent to investment.
- **Natural disasters:** extreme weather such as hurricanes, tornadoes, droughts and tsunamis can cause severe disruption to production of primary products, especially agricultural products.
- **Protectionism by developed countries:** for example, the huge subsidies given to US cotton farmers have created great difficulties for Indian cotton farmers, who are unable to compete; the EU's Common Agricultural Policy has meant that there is no free access to European markets for food from developing countries.
- **Low income elasticity of demand for primary products:** the **Prebisch–Singer hypothesis** states that the **terms of trade** between primary products and manufactured goods tend to deteriorate over time.

The Prebisch–Singer hypothesis

This theory suggests that countries that export commodities would be able to import less and less for a given level of exports. Prebisch and Singer examined data over a long period of time and found the data suggested that the terms of trade for primary commodity exporters *did* have a tendency to decline. A common explanation for this is that the income elasticity of demand for manufactured goods is greater than that for primary products, especially food. Therefore, as incomes rise, the demand for manufactured goods increases more rapidly than demand for primary products and the prices of manufactured goods rise relative to the prices of primary products, so causing a decline in the terms of trade for countries dependent on the export of primary products.

The theory may be criticised on the following grounds.
- First, some countries have developed on the basis of their primary products (e.g. Botswana: diamonds).
- Second, if a developing country has a comparative advantage in a primary product, then its resources will be used more efficiently by specialising in the production of that product.
- Third, primary product prices rose sharply until the middle of 2008 while the prices of many manufactured products were falling.

Some economists argue that, in the case of food, prices are likely to increase as world population grows and incomes in countries such as China and India rise, so causing higher demand for many foods traditionally eaten by those in developed countries.

Similarly, the outlook for countries such as Bolivia is good. Nearly half the world's known reserves of lithium (which can be used to make batteries for hybrid and electric vehicles) are located in Bolivia. Given the decline in oil production and subsidies being given to companies to develop electric cars, demand for lithium can be expected to rise sharply in the future.

In contrast, countries producing and exporting copper, such as Chile, were faced with a 50% fall in price between the middle of 2008 and 2009.

Knowledge check 19

Why is the demand for most primary products income inelastic?

Examiner tip

Always be prepared to include some theoretical models in your analysis. Evaluation is then possible by reference to real examples.

Savings gap

Many developing countries a have low GDP per capita and consequently they hold inadequate savings to finance the investment seen as essential to achieve economic growth and development. Figure 15 illustrates the problem.

Knowledge check 20
Is the value of the marginal propensity to save likely to be high or low in poor countries?

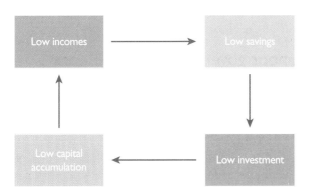

Figure 15 The cycle of problems due to low GDP per capita

Foreign exchange gap

Associated with the savings gap, many developing countries face a shortage of foreign exchange. This may be the result of a variety of factors including:
- dependence on export earnings from primary products
- dependence on imports of capital goods and other manufactured goods
- servicing debt
- capital flight

Capital flight

This occurs when individuals or companies decide to place cash deposits in foreign banks or buy shares or other assets in foreign countries. This has serious implications, for example:
- it contributes to the savings gap and foreign currency gap, and consequently ...
- it restricts economic growth
- it reduces the tax base because the country loses any tax payable on these assets

Debt

Many developing countries borrowed money at times of low interest rates, only to find that they were struggling to service the debt (pay the interest on it) some years later. Debt has become a problem for a variety of reasons including:
- risky decisions to borrow money to finance major investment projects at times when the world economy was strong and/or the prices of the goods which they were exporting were high
- an increase in oil prices, which presented particular problems over the periods of such price increases

- a fall in the value of the currencies of developing countries, which increased the burden of foreign debt
- loans taken out to finance expenditure on military equipment

When considering debt, it is important to remember that the absolute size of the debt is less important than a country's ability to finance it. This may be measured by examining data on debt service payments as a percentage of GDP or debt service payments as a percentage of export earnings.

Corruption, poor governance and civil wars

Corruption is usually defined as the use of power for personal gain. It may take a variety of forms including bribery, extortion and diversion of resources to the governing elite. Corruption acts as a constraint on development when it causes an inefficient allocation of resources.

Poor governance implies that the rulers of a country have adopted policies that result in the country's resources being allocated inefficiently. Government failure (where government intervention results in a net welfare loss) might also be evident as part of poor governance.

Civil wars, such as those that have occurred in Sudan and the Democratic Republic of the Congo, disrupt growth and development. Indeed, in so far as they actually cause destruction of infrastructure and the death of many people, they might negate any progress made in previous years.

All the above issues can deter both domestic investment and foreign direct investment and so limit the possibilities for growth and development.

Population issues

Population growth is particularly rapid in some of the poorest countries of the world such as Malawi and Mozambique. Meanwhile, population is falling in some developed countries such as Italy and Germany.

Population growth may be analysed in relation to the views of Thomas Malthus, who predicted at the end of the eighteenth century that famine was inevitable because population grows in geometric progression, whereas food production grows in the form of an arithmetic progression. Although his predictions were proved to be incorrect for Britain in the nineteenth century, some economists believe that they are still relevant for some of the poorest developing countries. In these countries the growth of the population is greater than the growth in GDP, with the result that GDP per capita is falling.

Human capital inadequacies

A country whose education standards are poor and where there is a low school enrolment ratio is likely to experience a slow rate of economic growth because the productivity of the workforce will be low. It will also act as a deterrent to transnational companies to invest in the country because of the costs involved in educating and training workers.

A particular problem for some countries is the prevalence of HIV and AIDS; when an adult develops AIDS, he or she may be forced to give up work. This means that the children might be withdrawn from school, either because the school fees can no longer be afforded or because they are required to work at home. A further problem arises if it is the teachers who contract AIDS, forcing them to give up work. The training of workers may also be disrupted by AIDS, particularly if a transnational company is involved and it decides that it is no longer profitable to operate in the country. The combined effect of these problems is to reduce the quantity and quality of education and training.

Poor infrastructure

Infrastructure covers the whole range of structures that are essential for an economy to operate smoothly. Infrastructure includes the following:

↓ reduces labor mobility

- transport
- telecommunications
- energy supply
- water supply
- waste disposal

Clearly, poor infrastructure will make it difficult to attract both domestic and foreign investment and thus present a significant obstacle to growth and development. On the other hand, a country rich in a natural resource demanded by other countries might benefit from foreign direct investment; a transnational company might provide some infrastructure to the country in order to facilitate its business investment, e.g. new roads, thus benefiting the whole country.

Examiner tip

It is very useful to have case study examples to include in your answers to illustrate these constraints on growth and development.

Summary

- There is a range of factors that might restrict growth and development in developing countries, one of the most significant of which is primary product dependency. This may be analysed by reference to the Prebisch–Singer hypothesis.

- Other factors limiting growth and development include: insufficient saving and foreign currency; capital flight; debt; corruption; civil wars; rapid population growth; poor human capital and infrastructure.

Examination skills and concepts
- Understanding the complex nature of economic development and its distinction from economic growth.
- Understanding the significance of problems associated with primary product dependency.
- Understanding the significance of the savings gap and foreign exchange gap.

Common examination errors
- Confusing economic growth with economic development.
- Inability to explain indicators of economic and social development.

Linkages and common themes
- Price elasticity of demand and income elasticity of demand when discussing primary product dependency (see Unit 1).
- Government failure (see Unit 1).

Strategies to promote growth and development

A range of strategies may be used to promote growth and development but there is no one simple prescription: each country is individual, having a different history, geography and natural resources. Consequently, policies which may appear to have worked in one country will not be successful in another country. In practice, it is likely that a combination of strategies may be required, with the particular blend being dependent on the characteristics and needs of that country. Various strategies are outlined below. As with the previous section, the emphasis is on developing countries but some of these strategies may also be relevant to developed economies. Figure 16 summarises these strategies.

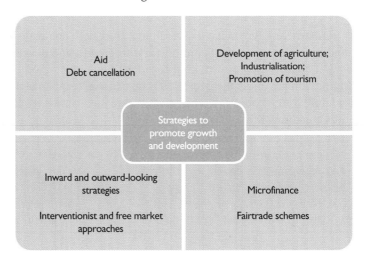

Figure 16 Strategies for growth and development

Examiner tip
Do not confuse aid with foreign direct investment.

Aid

The term 'aid' is used to describe the voluntary transfer of resources from one country to another or to loans given on concessionary terms (i.e. at less than the market rate of interest). Official development assistance (ODA) relates specifically to aid provided by governments and it excludes aid given by voluntary agencies. Aid may also be given for emergency relief (e.g. in the case of natural disasters or for the support of refugees during a civil war). This kind of aid is not usually contentious and so the focus here is on aid given for more general purposes.

The UN goal for the amount of aid offered by developed countries (agreed in 1970) is 0.7% of GDP.

There are various types of aid:
- **tied aid:** this is aid with conditions attached (e.g. there might be a requirement to buy goods from the donor country or the aid might be given on condition that there are some economic and political reforms)
- **bilateral aid:** aid given directly by one country to another

- **multilateral aid:** this occurs when countries pay money to an international agency which then distributes it to countries on the basis of certain criteria

Knowledge check 22

What is the difference between aid and FDI?

The arguments for aid

These include:
- the reduction in **absolute poverty**
- filling the **savings gap** experienced by many developing countries (this may be related to the **Harrod–Domar model)**
- providing funds for infrastructure — essential if the country is to industrialise. Aid, therefore, will help to increase **aggregate demand** and investment will have a **multiplier** effect on GDP. In turn, this will help to promote **sectoral development.**
- improving **human capital** through promotion of healthcare, education, training and expertise (e.g. the training of teachers and doctors). In some countries, aid might be used to help the prevention and treatment of AIDS.
- aid might **contribute to increased globalisation and trade**, both of which are frequently associated with growth and development.
- the reduction of world inequality

The arguments against aid

There are powerful arguments against the use of aid, except in the case of emergency aid, some of which are listed below:
- It results in a **dependency culture** (i.e. the recipients of aid become dependent on it and do not therefore pursue appropriate macroeconomic policies to achieve independent growth and development).
- Aid might not benefit those for whom it is intended (e.g. it could be diverted into military expenditure or it could be 'lost' as a result of **corruption**).
- There is no clear evidence that aid contributes to the reduction of absolute poverty or to growth and development.
- Right-wing economists argue that aid distorts market forces and results in an inefficient allocation of resources, while left-wing economists regard aid as a form of economic imperialism by which donor countries aim to secure political influence in the countries to which they give aid.
- Aid in the form of concessional loans involves the repayment of interest, in which case there will be an opportunity cost for the developing countries, e.g. improvements in the health and education services.

Debt cancellation

The burden of debt bears heavily on some countries, e.g. the Gambia, Mali, Nicaragua, Bolivia and Malawi.

The debt is usually owed to all or some of the following: the IMF, the World Bank, governments and banks in the developed countries.

The problem is that servicing the debt may account for a disproportionate amount of public expenditure, to the extent that resources available for expenditure on health and education are severely limited. As a result, pressure to cancel the debts of the poorest countries has increased. Under the Heavily Indebted Poor Countries (HIPC) initiative and the Multilateral Debt Relief Initiative (MDRI), the World Bank provides

debt relief to the poorest countries of the world. The HIPC initiative was started in 1996 by the IMF and World Bank with the aim of reducing the external debts of the poorest and most heavily indebted countries of the world to sustainable levels. Changes were made in 1999 to make the process quicker and deeper and to strengthen the links between debt relief poverty reduction and social policies. In 2005, the HIPC initiative was enhanced by the MDRI in order to speed up progress towards meeting the Millennium Development Goals (MDGs). Forty-one countries were identified as being eligible for HIPC initiative assistance and by the end of March 2009, 35 countries had benefited from HIPC debt relief.

Arguments for the cancellation of debt

These arguments include the following:

- Developing countries would have more foreign currency with which to buy imported capital and consumer goods from the developed countries.
- To the extent that the money released from debt cancellation is used for the purchase of capital goods, then there is the prospect of higher economic growth in the future.
- In turn, this means that developing countries would be able to buy more goods from richer countries.
- It would help to reduce absolute poverty.
- It would help to reduce both **the savings gap** and **foreign exchange gap.**
- It might help to conserve the environment, e.g. 'debt for nature swaps'.

Arguments against the cancellation of debt

These arguments include the following:

- In comparison with aid, it is likely to take much longer to agree a debt cancellation programme.
- Unless conditions are attached to debt cancellation, there is no guarantee that the governments of these countries will pursue sound macroeconomic policies (i.e. there a **moral hazard** problem).
- **Corruption** might mean that the benefits of debt cancellation are channelled to government officials rather than to the poor.
- Shareholders of banks in the developed world may bear some of the burden of debt cancellation.
- It may be much less effective than the introduction of policies to reduce protectionism in developed countries.

Development of different sectors of the economy

Agriculture

The problem associated with primary product dependency and agriculture in particular, was discussed in the previous section. However, some developing countries have achieved growth and development on the basis of investing in agriculture. The case for focusing on agriculture is that the country may have a comparative advantage in the production of agricultural goods and so resources are more efficiently allocated to that use. Such a comparative advantage should be viewed in a dynamic context (i.e. as the country experiences growth, the government may use its tax revenues to spend

Knowledge check 23

What is meant by debt servicing and why is it significant?

Knowledge check 24

Why might there be a moral hazard problem if debts of developing countries are cancelled?

Examiner tip

The arguments for and against debt cancellation are very similar to those for aid.

on education). As a result, the country may gain a comparative advantage in other products in the future.

Some countries have specialised in producing agricultural products with a high income elasticity of demand, e.g. Peru produces asparagus; Chile produces blueberries, wine and papaya. Consequently, during periods of world economic growth, they have benefited from significant increases in demand.

Manufacturing industry

It has traditionally been assumed that development is synonymous with industrialisation, i.e. that development requires an increasingly large manufacturing sector. The structural change/dual sector model (the **Lewis model**) is based on the view that development requires a move away from traditional agriculture (characterised by subsistence, low productivity and barter) to more productive manufacturing (characterised by high productivity and monetary exchange).

Key features of the Lewis model

- This model describes the transfer of surplus labour from a low productivity (subsistence) agricultural sector to a high productivity industrial sector.
- Lewis thought that, because of the excess supply of workers, the marginal productivity (MP) of agricultural workers might be zero or close to zero. This is based on the **law of diminishing returns**.
- With MP zero, then the opportunity cost of transferring workers from the agricultural sector to the industrial sector would be zero.
- Industrialisation will be associated with investment (possibly from transnational companies), which will increase productivity and profitability. If profits are reinvested, then further growth will occur.
- The share of profits as a percentage of GDP will increase, as will the savings ratio, providing more funds for investment and continued economic growth.

Criticisms of the Lewis model

- Profits made in the industrial sector might not be invested locally, especially if firms are owned by transnational companies.
- Reinvestment might be made in capital equipment, with the result that extra labour is not required.
- Empirical evidence suggests that the assumption of surplus labour in the agricultural sector and full employment in the industrial sector is invalid, e.g. favelas in South America.

Tourism

Some countries have developed on the basis of investment in tourism. Clearly there are advantages to this strategy over primary product dependency, not least that demand is likely to be **income elastic.** The expansion of tourism has strong attractions for developing countries.

Advantages of tourism

It is a valuable source of foreign currency as tourists spend money on goods and services provided within the local economy.

Examiner tip
Think critically about whether industrialisation is essential for economic development.

Knowledge check 25
Define the law of diminishing returns.

- Tourism is likely to attract investment by transnational hotel chains.
- In turn, this will increase GDP via the multiplier.
- Jobs will be created, both as a direct result of the investment in the tourist and leisure industries and also as a result of the multiplier effects within the economy.
- All of the above will help to increase tax revenues for the government, which may be used to improve public services.
- It can help to preserve the national heritage of the country.
- Improvements in infrastructure may be made (e.g. a transnational company provides new roads as part of its contract to build hotels).

Drawbacks of tourism

There are some serious drawbacks associated with tourism:
- It may be associated with a significant increase in imports, not only for the capital equipment required to build hotels and facilities but also to meet the demands of tourists for specialist foods and goods. Further, the balance of payments might be adversely affected by the repatriation of profits to shareholders of TNCs.
- In times of recession, the fall in demand may be more than proportionate, assuming that demand is income elastic.
- Employment may only be seasonal in nature. Further, the jobs created may only be low skilled and low paid if the TNC supplies its own managers and professional staff.
- Tourism is subject to changes in fashion. In the developed world, Spain has suffered from a significant downturn in tourism in recent years, as Europeans now prefer more exotic destinations.
- There may be significant **external costs** (e.g. increase in waste, pollution of beaches, water shortages for local people) as the needs of tourists are prioritised. The damage to the environment caused by tourists might result in restrictions (e.g. the restrictions on the number of tourists allowed each day on the Galapagos islands; visitors to Machu Picchu are limited by the requirement to have a guide).

Examiner tip
Promotion of tourism is just one of many areas in this unit where concepts learned in previous units may be applied, for example: multiplier; AD/AS diagrams; balance of payments; income elasticity of demand; external costs.

Sectoral balance

It is sometimes argued that dependence on the growth of just one of the above sectors results in sectoral imbalance. This may limit the growth and development of the whole economy because the country may become too dependent on one product. This is undesirable because of sudden changes in demand or supply. Further, a lack of investment might cause a fall in productivity in the other sectors. However, if a country has a comparative advantage in that product or sector, then such specialisation might be desirable.

Inward-looking and outward-looking strategies

The strategies adopted by countries to construct a path towards diversification and industrialisation have taken a variety of forms.

Inward-looking strategies are characterised by:
- **import substitution** (i.e. replacement of imports with domestically produced manufactured goods)
- **protectionism**

The aim of inward-looking strategies is to enable a country to diversify in a controlled way until it has built a strong domestic base. Clearly, this approach will be most effective where a country's domestic market is large enough to enable industries to benefit from economies of scale. Once achieved, industry will be strong enough to cope with foreign competition.

However, there are some drawbacks to this approach:
- **comparative advantage** is distorted and so resources will not be allocated efficiently
- the **lack of competition** could result in inefficiency

In contrast, outward-looking strategies are characterised by:
- free trade
- deregulation of capital markets
- promotion of foreign direct investment (FDI)
- devaluation of exchange rates

The disadvantages of these policies have been considered in previous sections. In practice, many countries have used a combination of strategies.

Interventionist and free market approaches

Interventionist strategies

For at least 30 years after the Second World War, most developing countries experienced significant degrees of government intervention. This approach was characterised by the following:
- import substitution policies
- nationalisation
- farmers forced to sell their produce to state-controlled boards at low prices
- price subsidies on many goods regarded as necessities
- over-valued exchange rates (aimed at keeping down the cost of imports)

By the end of the 1970s, there was increasing disillusion with such interventionist policies, which were associated with:
- low rates of economic growth
- resource and allocative inefficiency because of the absence of the profit motive
- government failure
- corruption by civil servants associated with increased government intervention
- increasing fiscal deficits (associated with subsidies and nationalised industries)
- increasing balance of payments deficits on current account (associated with over-valued currencies)

Free market approaches

The perceived failure of interventionist strategies and the election of right-wing governments in the USA and UK resulted in the adoption of free market and outward-looking strategies. The key components of these strategies are:
- **free market analysis:** assumes markets are efficient and therefore the best way to allocate resources
- **public choice theory:** based on the assumption that politicians, civil servants and governments use their power for their own self interest

Knowledge check 26
Identify four disadvantages of FDI.

Examiner tip
The benefits and problems associated with FDI may be analysed by reference to the impact on the balance of payments; employment; economic growth and sustainability; tax revenues; and exploitation of resources.

In particular, the free market approach is characterised by:

- trade liberalisation
- market liberalisation
- supply-side policies
- structural adjustment programmes

Since the turn of the decade there has been some modification to this approach in recognition of the fact that imperfections exist in product and labour markets, for example:

- asymmetric information
- externalities
- absence of property rights (Hernando de Soto)
- investment decisions

There is, therefore, a need for governments to intervene in a market-friendly way (e.g. by investing in infrastructure, education, health) and to provide a favourable climate for enterprise.

Microfinance

Microfinance is a means of providing extremely poor families with small loans (microcredit) to help them engage in productive activities or grow their tiny businesses. In particular, it can help the poor to increase income, build businesses and reduce vulnerability to external shocks.

The pioneer of microfinance was Mohammed Yunus, who established the Grameen Bank in Bangladesh.

The key features of microfinance schemes are as follows:

- In contrast to development lending, microcredit insists on repayment.
- Interest is charged to cover the costs involved.
- The focus is on groups whose alternative sources of finance are limited to the informal sector, where the interest charged would be high.

The main clients of microfinance are:

- women (who form more than 97% of the clients)
- the self-employed, often household-based entrepreneurs
- small farmers in rural areas
- small shopkeepers, street vendors and service providers in urban areas

Criticisms of microfinance

Concerns have been raised about the repayment rate, collection methods and questionable accounting practices.

On a larger scale, some argue that an overemphasis on microfinance to combat poverty will lead to a reduction of other assistance to the poor, such as official development assistance or aid from non-government organisations.

Fair trade

The aim of fair trade schemes is 'to address the injustice of low prices' by guaranteeing that producers receive a fair price. It means paying producers an above–market price for their produce, provided they meet particular labour and production standards. This premium is passed back to the producers to spend on development programmes.

The market for fair trade products has been growing rapidly and there are now over 2,500 product lines, including chocolate, tea, coffee, bananas, wine and clothes.

Benefits of fair trade schemes

- Producers receive a higher price.
- Extra money is available to spend on education, health, infrastructure, clean water supplies, conversion to organic farming and other development programmes in the producers' countries.
- There are smaller price fluctuations, allowing producers to be shielded from market forces.
- The extra money can also be used to improve the quality of products.
- Producers are enabled to diversify into other products.

Criticisms of fair trade schemes

- Distortion of market forces: low prices are due to overproduction and producers ought to recognise this as a signal to switch to growing other crops. Further, the artificially high prices encourage more producers to enter the market.
- Certification is based on normative views on the best way to organise labour, e.g. in the case of coffee, certification is only available to cooperatives of small producers.
- Guaranteeing a minimum price provides no incentive to improve quality.
- It is an inefficient way to get money to poor producers: consumers pay a large premium for fair trade goods but much of this goes to supermarkets in profits. Only 10% of the premium paid for fair trade coffee trickles down to the producer.
- It may create a dependency trap for producers.

Knowledge check 28

Why is free trade sometimes regarded as being unfair to producers in developing countries?

The role of international financial institutions

The International Monetary Fund

The original role of the International Monetary Fund (IMF) was to increase international liquidity and to provide stability in capital markets through a system of convertible currencies pegged to the dollar. It also lent to countries with temporary balance of payments deficits on current account.

In the 1970s, there were significant oil price shocks and many countries — especially developing countries — suffered from rapid inflation, huge balance of payments deficits and debt crises. As a result, most currencies were allowed to float (i.e. the peg to the dollar was broken). The IMF extended its role to include involvement in economic development and poverty reduction. To ensure repayment of loans, the IMF imposed restrictions and conditions on the economic policies to be followed by developing countries — **stabilisation programmes** — to achieve internal and external balance. In practice, these were similar to **structural adjustment programmes** (see below).

In 2006, the IMF was given a new role; namely, to conduct multilateral surveillance of the global economy and to suggest steps that the leading nations should take to

promote it. It was also required to ensure more balanced growth and to reduce global imbalances

The IMF is funded by quotas from countries, based on their GDP. Up to a quarter of the quota is payable in dollars, euros, yen or sterling or Special Drawing Rights (SDR) and the other three-quarters in the country's own currency. The value of an SDR is defined as the value of a fixed amount of yen, dollars, pounds and euros, expressed in dollars at the current exchange rate. These SDRs represent a potential claim on other countries' foreign currency reserves, for which they can be exchanged voluntarily. In December 2010, it was agreed that IMF's quota resources would be doubled in order to deal with expected new demands resulting from the sovereign debt crisis.

The IMF can also borrow on the basis of the 'New Arrangements to Borrow' and the 'General Agreement to Borrow'. These provide the possibility of accessing about $580 billion in the event of a major financial crisis.

Knowledge check 29

What has been the role of the IMF in helping countries with sovereign debt crises?

The International Bank for Reconstruction and Development (IBRD)

More commonly known as the World Bank, its original role was to provide long-term loans for reconstruction and development to member nations that had suffered in the Second World War.

In the 1970s, its role changed to setting up agricultural reforms in developing countries, giving loans and providing expertise.

In 1982, Mexico defaulted on its loan repayments. As a result, the World Bank now imposes structural adjustment programmes (SAPs), which set out the conditions on which loans are given. The aim is to ensure that debtor countries do not default on the repayment of debts.

SAPs were based on free market reforms (e.g. trade liberalisation, removal of state subsidies on food, privatisation and reduction in public expenditure to reduce budget deficits). However, these free market reforms were criticised because they:
- did little to help the world's poor
- failed to promote development
- increased inequality
- caused environmental degradation
- resulted in social and political chaos in many countries

The widespread criticism of SAPs and the devastating effect which they had on some developing countries resulted in the World Bank changing its focus to concentrate on poverty reduction strategies, with aid being directed towards:
- countries following sound macroeconomic policies
- healthcare; broadening education
- local communities rather than central governments

Examiner tip

Use case study material in your examination answers. The World Bank website (www.worldbank.org) provides detailed information on countries.

The future of the IMF and World Bank

The roles of the IMF and the World Bank are currently blurred: both have a role in the developing world and in poverty reduction and it is suggested that they should be reformed to reflect the changing needs of the global economy. Critics of the institutions as they currently operate suggest the following:

- The IMF should be slimmed down and should undertake short-term lending to crisis–hit countries.
- The World Bank should act as a development agency and undertake a detailed credit appraisal of the creditworthiness of recipient countries.

The role of non-government organisations

The work of non-government organisations (NGOs) has brought **community-based development** to the forefront of strategies to promote growth and development (i.e. the focus has moved away from state managed schemes). The key characteristics of these community-based schemes are:

- local control of small-scale projects
- self reliance
- emphasis on using the skills available
- environmental sustainability

Summary

- There are many ways by which developing countries could achieve growth and development, including: aid; debt cancellation; industrialisation; development of tourism; inward and outward-looking strategies; interventionist and free market approaches; microfinance; and fair trade schemes.
- Obviously other factors can play an important role, such as the development of human capital and improvements of infrastructure, but these usually come from other sources, e.g. aid or as a result of FDI by transnational companies. It should be remembered that the governments of many developing countries do not have the resources to finance these themselves.
- The IMF, World Bank and Non-Government Organisations can play an important role in promoting growth and development.

Examination skills and concepts

- Ability to evaluate a range of strategies to promote growth and development.
- Ability to give examples from specific countries to illustrate the points made.
- Evaluation of the roles of the IMF and World Bank and how they might change.

Common examination errors

- Confusion between aid and FDI.
- Assumption that measures to increase economic growth will automatically result in development.

Linkages and common themes

- In discussing the strategies, it is often appropriate to employ *AD/AS* analysis, e.g. in considering the impact of aid (see Unit 2).
- The free market approach links with the market economics covered in Unit 1.

Questions & Answers

This section contains two essay and two data–response questions, together with sample answers, which are designed to help your learning, revision and examination preparation. The questions are of a style similar to that which you can expect in the examination, although it is possible that the mark allocations for the data–response questions and number of parts could vary.

For each question you will find:

- a sample student answer
- examiner's comments on each essay and data–response question explaining, where relevant, how the response could be improved and a higher grade achieved. Comments on the questions are preceded by the icon ⓔ. Comments on student answers are preceded by the icon ⓔ.

These questions are likely to be of greatest use if you answer the questions yourself under timed conditions before you read the sample answer and examiner's comment. Remember to include diagrams wherever relevant and integrate them into your written analysis.

Exam format

Unit 4 makes up 60% of the total marks for A2 (30% of the total A-level mark. It is worth a maximum of 120 UMS marks (UMS stands for 'uniform mark score', which scales your actual mark to one that by statistical correction makes it equivalent to any other exam). It is important to note that your mark for this unit will make a significant contribution to your overall grade for the subject.

The examination has two sections: essays and data response. Section A consists of three essays, each in two parts, the first part worth 20 marks and the second worth 30 marks, making a total of 50. Students are required to answer one essay from this section. In Section B there is a choice between two data–response questions, each of which has five parts. The data–response question is also worth 50 marks, so the raw mark for this paper is 100.

Assessment objectives

There are four assessment objectives in each unit of the AS and A-level economics, namely **knowledge**, **application**, **analysis** and **evaluation**. In this unit, the higher order skills of analysis and evaluation carry more weight than in any of the other units.

Objective	Assessment objectives	Weighting
1	Knowledge and understanding: demonstrate knowledge and understanding of the specified content	20%
2	Application: apply knowledge and understanding of the specified content to problems and issues arising from both familiar and unfamiliar situations	20%
3	Analysis: analyse economic problems and issues	30%
4	Evaluation: evaluate economic arguments and evidence, making informed judgements	30%

The command words used in the questions should give a clear indication as to which skills are being tested. It is essential that you understand the meaning behind these words, so that you are sure about what is being expected. Some of the key command words are defined on page 59.

Knowledge and understanding

This objective involves the ability to define key words and terms, together with an ability to understand the economic theories and models that you are expected to use in the examination. In Unit 4, you should be able to define terms that you have learned from previous units, as well as concepts such as globalisation, international competitiveness, balance of payment deficit/surplus on current account, real exchange rate, fiscal surplus/deficit and economic development.

Application

This assessment objective may be demonstrated by an ability to apply knowledge and understanding to particular contexts. It is likely that essays and, more especially, data–response questions will be set in a real world context so generalised responses are unlikely to score highly.

Analysis

Analysis is a multi-stage process and therefore involves developing a logical line of argument in a series of steps. This skill (along with evaluation) is particularly important in answering questions on this unit, so practice is essential. Typically, analysis is likely to involve drawing a diagram (such as an aggregate-demand/aggregate-supply diagram) and then explaining the changes that have occurred. For example, a question might require analysis of how a recession in the USA might impact on other countries; how a significant change in commodity prices affects the global economy or how a dramatic depreciation of one country's currency might affect that country's economy and those of its major trading partners.

Evaluation

This objective requires you to demonstrate a critical approach to the subject/data under consideration. This is a challenging task but since evaluation carries 30% of the total marks on this unit, it vital to ensure that this skill is demonstrated where required. In the context of Unit 4, for both parts of the essay and at least three parts of the data–response questions, the first issue is to detect when evaluation is required. The command word is the key. Any question using any of the following command words implies that evaluation must be included: **examine; assess; evaluate; to what extent; discuss; comment upon.** The second issue is to devise strategies for evaluation, which could include the following:

- short- and long-run effects
- the magnitude of an effect
- questioning the validity of the assumptions behind a theory or model
- the reliability and validity of the data
- missing information
- advantages and disadvantages of an argument
- differential effects on different stakeholders
- prioritising the effects in terms of the most/least significant

Grade boundaries

Obviously you will be aiming high, so the performance descriptors for the A/B boundary as formulated by all the examination boards are given below. Further comments *in italics* are made by the author of this guide.

Knowledge

Candidates characteristically demonstrate:

- detailed knowledge of a range of facts and concepts
- clear understanding of terminology, institutions and models
- detailed knowledge and clear understanding of the interconnections between the different elements of the subject content

Essentially you must be able to include precise definitions in your answers, identify key points relevant to the question and know relevant information about the global economy.

Application

Candidates characteristically apply concepts; numerical and graphical techniques and terminology to complex issues arising in familiar and unfamiliar situations.

You must be able to support your essay answers by including relevant examples and make effective use of the information provided in the data questions. This may involve calculations and illustrating your answer with diagrams.

Analysis

Candidates characteristically:

- select relevant concepts, models, theories and techniques
- demonstrate, for the most part, development of logical explanations for complex economic problems and issues, with focus and relevance

This involves using the economist's toolbox of concepts, models and theories and explaining the steps of an argument in a logical way. Remember that analysis is a multi-stage process requiring a detailed breakdown of how, for example, a change in the availability of credit will work through the economy.

Evaluation

Candidates characteristically evaluate complex economic arguments:
- prioritise evidence and arguments
- make reasoned arguments
- reach and present supported conclusions
- make reasoned recommendations

Typically, a good piece of evaluation will involve a critical approach to the question which demonstrates that rarely in economics will there be an unequivocal answer to a question.

Key command words

Define: you should give a clear and precise meaning of a term or concept.

Explain: you should give reasons for a particular situation or changes in a variable.

Analyse: requires you to give a multi-stage process of explanation including identification of assumptions; relevant diagrams; and a step-by-step account of, for example, how a change in a variable might impact on different economic agents.

Evaluate, **examine**, **assess**, **discuss** and **to what extent:** all these are evaluative command words that require you to offer critical appraisal of a situation or of the potential effects of a change in a variable. Evaluation may be demonstrated by examination of issues such as the magnitude of the change; the time frame under which the effects will occur (i.e. short-run and long-run effects); the advantages and disadvantages of the change; the relative importance of the factors identified; consideration of the reliability and validity of the data provided; identification of missing information which might make a judgement difficult; the realism of the assumptions made.

How to answer essay questions

You have a choice of one out of three essays. Each essay is split into two parts, part (a) being worth 20 marks and part (b) being worth 30 marks. You will have 1 hour to answer this section of the paper but it is advisable to spend 50 minutes actually writing your answer. This leaves 10 minutes for planning your answer and for checking your response at the end.

Both parts require evaluation, so you need to adopt a critical approach to the question.

Here are some further tips for writing essays:
- **Select your question carefully.** In particular, ensure that you are able to answer both parts of the question and that you are able to apply relevant economic analysis.
- **Plan your answer.** Write down key words or phrases that will form the basis of the paragraphs or draw a mind map indicating the areas that you intend to cover. This approach might enable you to think more broadly: all too often essay answers are focused too narrowly. In part (a) questions, you should consider at least three points/issues/factors and for part (b) questions, you should discuss at least four points/issues/factors.
- **Define key concepts and terms in the question.** It will quickly become apparent to an examiner if you are uncertain about a concept, so it is better to explain the concepts and terms precisely in your introductory paragraph.

- **Apply economic concepts and theories wherever possible.** Remember that this is a synoptic unit, so you need to demonstrate your facility with concepts learned from different parts of the specification, both micro and macro.
- **Practise your analytical writing skills.** Remember that analysis is a multi-stage process, so practise the skill of developing logical and carefully reasoned answers. For example, consider the implications of the withdrawal of foreign direct investment on a country's economy.
- **Include diagrammatic analysis.** This unit provides considerable scope for including aggregate-demand/aggregate-supply analysis especially in the context of international economics; the application of monetary, fiscal and supply-side policies; and foreign direct investment. However, there is also the opportunity of using production possibility frontiers, e.g. in the context of comparative advantage as well as microeconomic supply and demand diagrams (perhaps in the context of tariffs or to illustrate the causes of changes in commodity prices in the context of developing countries).
- **Use your knowledge about current economic issues.** Both the essays and data–response questions usually provide an opportunity to demonstrate your knowledge about current issues. Generalised answers and those based solely on a theoretical approach are unlikely to secure the highest marks.
- **Allocate your time carefully.** In effect, you have 1 hour for the essay. Each essay is split into two parts, part (a) worth 20 marks and part (b) worth 30 marks. This provides a simple but useful guide to the division of your time: spend about 20 minutes writing your answer to part (a) and 30 minutes to part (b). This will leave 10 minutes for planning your answer and for checking your response at the end. Avoid spending more than 1 hour on the essay, otherwise you will leave yourself insufficient time to answer the data–response questions fully.
- **Evaluate.** It is a good idea to evaluate the issues discussed in each paragraph. It is also useful to include an evaluative conclusion at the end of your answer to each part of the question.
- **Practise.** Writing an essay under timed conditions is a challenge. It is easy to lose focus, spend too much time on the first part of the essay or not write in a structured, logical manner. Effort spent practising writing essays can, therefore, really enhance your examination performance. It is a good idea to start by writing an answer to a question that you have already planned and then go on to tackle unfamiliar questions.

How to answer data–response questions

You have a choice between two data–response questions and each question consists of five parts. Those with an asterisk indicate that they will be used to assess 'quality of written communication'. In the specimen papers, three of the five parts demand evaluation, so take particular care to ensure that you spot the evaluation command words. As with the essay, 50 marks are allocated to the data–response question so you should allocate 1 hour for your answer.

All data used for these questions are drawn from published sources so frequent reading of articles related to economics will pay considerable dividends. Among the most common sources for questions used in examination papers are the Economist, the Financial Times, The Times, the Independent, the Guardian and the Daily Telegraph.

Here are some further tips for answering data–response questions:

- **Select your question carefully.** To make your selection, it is advisable to start by reading through the *questions* rather than the data material. This will ensure that you select the question on which you are likely to score most highly. Only then should you read through all the data material attached to the questions.
- **Check graphs and data.** To avoid making mistakes in interpretation of graphs and data, it is important to:
  - check the axis titles
  - look at the scale of the charts
  - identify possible trends. In this context it may be useful to calculate percentage changes because these are often more meaningful than absolute changes.
  - consider whether the data are sufficient or whether other information would be helpful
  - question the validity or reliability of the data. Remember that selective use of data can give a very misleading picture.
- **Check the command words.** Not all the data questions will require evaluation, so be sure to look out for those that do.
- **Define key terms.** Remember that 20% of the marks available for this question are awarded for knowledge, so do not forget to define a key term which appears in the question or one which is pertinent in your answer.
- **Make use of the information provided.** There is a danger of writing generalised answers to the questions. To avoid this, ensure that appropriate use is made of the information provided because this could enable you to gain marks for application to the context. For example, it might be possible to do some simple calculations to demonstrate the changes in the size of a budget deficit.
- **Apply economic concepts and theories.** It should be possible to apply a wide range of concepts in your answers. As with the essays, appropriate use should be made of the *AD/AS* model and, in addition, concepts from previous units.
- **Include diagrammatic analysis.** Some questions might specifically require a diagram to be drawn, such as one illustrating the effects of a tariff. However, even where one is not specifically requested, there may be opportunities to include diagrams. These can be an invaluable part of your analysis, not least because they can reduce the amount that needs to be written. Nevertheless, it is important to integrate diagrams fully into your written analysis — do not just include a diagram without any reference to it in your response.
- **Plan your time carefully.** As a rough guide, the number of marks indicates the number of minutes that you should spend on each part. This allows 10 minutes for selection of question, reading the associated information and checking your answer at the end. A common mistake is for students to spend far too long answering questions which are worth relatively few marks leaving themselves insufficient time to answer the questions with larger mark bases.
- **Practise.** Completing a 50-mark data–response question under timed conditions presents various challenges, not least the danger of spending too much time on the initial questions at the expense of the later questions which carry higher marks. Practising the questions from the end of this book or from past examination papers will provide invaluable experience and enable you to enhance your skills.

Stretch and challenge and the A* grade

In devising the new assessments, the examination boards were required to ensure that there were opportunities for students to demonstrate the depth and breadth of their knowledge, understanding, analytical and evaluative skills. Broadly, this is achieved by setting essay questions which are open ended and having fewer parts to the data–response questions, so that students are not led through the answer.

Students able to demonstrate these skills could then be awarded an A* grade but the conditions required are extremely challenging: a score of 90% UMS must be achieved on the A2 units and at least 80% on the two AS units. On the basis of the previous specifications, only a small proportion of students are expected to be awarded A* grades.

Essay questions

Essay question 1 **Investment by transnational companies**

(a) Examine the reasons why a transnational company might wish to invest in a developing country.

(20 marks)

The answer could begin with a brief definition of a transnational company and then quickly proceed to identifying and explaining at least three possible reasons why a TNC might wish to invest in a developing country. Examples would be useful in illustrating the points made. Since the command word is 'examine', it is important to include some evaluative comments.

(b) Evaluate the potential impact on developing countries of inward investment by transnational companies.

(30 marks)

A useful approach to questions of this nature is to consider the impact on various macroeconomic objectives such as economic growth, employment, the balance of payments, inflation and the environment.

Student answer

(a) Investment by transnational companies is an example of foreign direct investment (FDI). Such investment increased significantly over the last 30 years, until the financial crisis brought a sharp reduction. However, the subsequent recovery has resulted in a recovery in FDI.

There are a number of factors which attract TNCs to set up factories in developing countries. First, and possibly most important, is the attraction of low labour costs. Labour costs are frequently the most significant cost of a business, especially those whose production is labour-intensive. In practice, the potential savings from shifting production from, say, the USA to China, easily outweigh the transport costs involved in sending the finished goods back to the USA. Unlike developed countries, few developing countries have national minimum wages, meaning that wage costs can be exceptionally low. **a**

Other costs may also be significantly lower in a developing country. For example, health and safety regulations and environmental regulations represent a considerable cost for firms in many developed countries but they may be nonexistent in developing countries. Both this factor and the access to cheap labour can help to increase the profits of TNCs and therefore provide an important motive for such investment.

TNCs may wish to establish themselves in developing countries so that they can gain access to new, fast-growing markets. In doing so, they may gain more economies of scale (reduction in long-run average costs). It may also be the case that the developing country could be part of a trading bloc, so that establishing itself in such a developing country would enable the TNC to secure access to that market without being subject to tariffs. **b**

Another factor which acts a major incentive for investment by TNCs in developing countries is the opportunity to exploit raw materials which may be present. This has been a significant factor behind Chinese investment in African countries, including Sudan. **c**

For the manufacture of components or production of manufactured goods, it is likely that labour costs will be the crucial factor influencing the decision by a TNC to invest in a developing country. However, there have been increasing investments by mining companies in developing countries keen to secure supplies of scarce raw materials. **d**

ⓔ **18/20 marks awarded. a** A good paragraph, which focuses on one of the key reasons for FDI. There is a hint of evaluation in the sentence beginning 'Labour costs are frequently the most significant cost of a business…' However, this could have been developed further to include reference to non-wage costs such as National Insurance. **b** A good point but it could have been illustrated by reference to specific countries – China and India being obvious examples. **c** Examples of raw materials would be a useful addition to this point. **d** This concluding paragraph illustrates that the motives for FDI may differ and, therefore, that it is not easy to select the most important factor. This would be considered as evaluation.

(b) Investment by TNCs is a component of aggregate demand and so there will be a rightward shift in the AD curve. Since investment is an injection, it will cause a multiplier effect on GDP (i.e. the initial investment will cause a more than proportionate rise in GDP). This multiplier effect could be quite large because the marginal propensity to consume in developing countries is often high. **a** In addition, this investment will help to increase the productive capacity of the country, thus causing a rightward shift in the long-run aggregate-supply curve. The figure below illustrates the effect on the inward investment on real output of the developing economy.

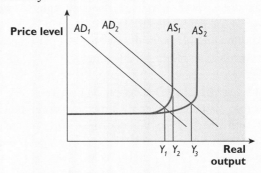

It can be seen that the initial effect of the increase in AD will be an increase in real output Y_1 to Y_2. In the longer term, there will be a further increase in real output from Y_2 to Y_3, resulting from the increase in long-run aggregate supply. The exact impact on real output will depend on the magnitude of the rise in AD and AS and on the gradient of the $LRAS$ curve (i.e. the initial impact of the rise in AD will have a greater impact on real output if the AS curve is elastic because of significant spare capacity in the economy). A problem with this economic growth is that external costs (costs imposed on third parties not part of the transaction) will increase too. For example, there may be more air pollution and greenhouse gases, so that production is above the socially optimal level. **b**

This investment and increased real income should bring an increase in employment in the developing country. However, the TNC may supply its own managers and skilled workers so that only jobs for low-skilled workers are created. Also, there is a danger of exploitation of workers (long hours or use of child labour). Further, domestic firms making similar products may be unable to compete and so go out of business. Therefore, the net effect on jobs might be quite small. **c**

FDI should result in increased tax revenues for the governments of developed countries (e.g. from income tax and corporation tax). With this extra revenue, the government can spend more on health, education and infrastructure. This should translate into increased development because there will be longer life expectancy and a higher quality workforce, which should be more productive. However, a major problem in many developing countries is corruption, so there is a danger that the extra tax revenues will not be used for development purposes but diverted into the hands of government officials or used for defence. **d**

The FDI will provide an inflow into the financial account of the balance of payments and once goods are being produced, exports will increase (because TNCs usually use the base of a developing country to export to the rest of the world), so benefiting the current account. These flows help to fill the foreign exchange gap faced by many developing countries that have insufficient foreign currency to service international debts and buy essential capital equipment and raw materials. However, in the long run, there may be an outflow from the current account in the form of interest, profits and dividends to the shareholders of the TNC.

There is a danger that the inward investment might result in an increase in inequality — the Gini coefficient would rise — because FDI is often focused on manufacturing in urban areas so the income gap between workers in rural and urban areas may increase. Also, those employed by the TNC may earn more than those employed by local firms. However, this increase in inequality may be offset by government measures such as progressive taxation. **e**

ⓔ **28/30 marks awarded a** A good start to this answer. However, the term 'marginal propensity to consume' could be explained, as well as the reason why its value may be high in developing countries. **b** Good analysis and evaluation of the diagram, followed by another evaluative point relating to the external costs of a higher rate of economic growth. **c** The impact of FDI on employment is explained and evaluated well. **d** A good paragraph but perhaps the concept of economic development could be included in the analysis, i.e. in an explanation of how increased tax revenues could promote development. **e** The final two paragraphs also contain sound analysis and the student's evaluative comments show evidence of his/her critical approach to the material.

ⓔ **Total score: 46/50 = grade A***

Essay question 2 Britain's trade in goods

(a) Britain's trade in goods deficit was over £81 billion in 2009. Discuss the view that Britain's trade in goods deficit is a reflection of a fundamental lack of competitiveness. (20 marks)

In the introductory paragraph, it is advisable to define the key terms in the question, namely 'trade in goods deficit' and competitiveness. Some reasons for the lack of competitiveness should then be considered, such as low productivity, the value of the pound sterling and non-price factors.

(b) Evaluate the view that exchange rate adjustment is all that is necessary to improve Britain's competitiveness. (30 marks)

An obvious way to begin this answer is a detailed explanation and evaluation of how a depreciation in the value of the pound might improve competitiveness of the UK's goods and services. This could then lead to a consideration of other methods by which competitiveness might be improved.

Student answer

(a) Competitiveness refers to the ability of a country to sell its goods internationally. It may be measured by considering relative productivity rates between countries, unit labour costs or using composite indices such as the global competitiveness index. **a**

Britain's trade in goods deficit has been declining steadily over the last 10 years and a variety of factors has contributed to this deterioration.

With regard to productivity, Britain has lower productivity than that of many of its major competitors but the productivity gap with other countries has been closing, so it does not provide a complete explanation for the deterioration in the trade in goods balance. Another measure of competitiveness is the real normalised unit labour costs (RNULC), which relate to labour costs adjusted for inflation and converted into a common currency to make international comparisons possible. It is likely that Britain's RNULC are higher than some of its competitors. In recent years, the trend has been for manufacturing firms to locate in areas such as the Far East, where labour costs are a fraction of UK levels. This has harmed the ability of the UK to compete on price in the trade in goods significantly. **b**

One of the most significant factors that might explain Britain's trade in goods deficit was the high value of the pound between 1996 and 2008. In particular, the pound was high relative to the euro. This is significant because a large proportion of Britain's trade is with EU countries. A strong pound has a negative effect on the price competitiveness of UK goods abroad while making foreign imports cheaper to UK consumers. **c** Provided that the combined price elasticity of demand for the UK's exports and imports exceeds unity (i.e. the Marshall–Lerner condition is met), these changes will worsen the UK's balance of trade in goods. However, the value of the pound was high partly because Britain had a strong economy relative to other countries and was successful in attracting foreign direct investment (which increases demand for sterling, so causing a rise in its value).

A further factor that could explain the trade in goods deficit was the high level of aggregate demand and economic growth up until the recession that began at the end of 2008. In particular, consumer spending was high (and the savings ratio low), with confidence high as a result of the buoyant housing market — until 2008. This tends to result in a worsening trade in goods balance because a large proportion of increases in consumer spending is inclined to be spent on imported goods. **d** Indeed, the UK's high marginal propensity to import is an important factor in explaining the trade in goods balance but this, in turn, is affected by non-price factors such as design, quality, reliability and availability, all of which affect competitiveness. **e**

(e) **13/20 marks awarded a** A good attempt at a definition of competitiveness, although it would be desirable to mention non-price factors also such as quality, design and reliability. However, these factors are mentioned at the end of the answer. **b** A sound definition and discussion of the significance of unit labour costs, which is related well to competitiveness. **c** The impact of the high value of the pound for competitiveness of the UK's goods and services is explained well and is followed by some relevant evaluation on price elasticity of demand for imports and exports. **d** The high level of aggregate demand is a good point and explained well. **e** A weakness of this answer is that there is insufficient evaluation, although the third point might be regarded as evaluative rather than a reason for a lack of competitiveness. There is no mention of how the recession in 2009 might have reduced the demand for imports, which could suggest that the deficit is only a short-term problem. Further, the UK's loss of comparative advantage in manufacturing to countries such as China is ignored.

(b) A depreciation in the value of sterling occurred in the latter half of 2008 and in the first few months of 2009. A direct result was that UK goods became cheaper in foreign markets and so improved their price competitiveness. **a** To benefit from this improvement in competitiveness, however, British firms must be able to meet the increased demand (i.e. supply needs to be elastic). Much depends on the availability of stocks and the flexibility of the labour market, so that output can be increased quickly. There are other dangers with such a depreciation. For example, it tends to spark inflation as imports — especially raw materials — rise in price. Consequently, a wage-price spiral might occur, with workers seeking to maintain their real incomes. Higher wages in the manufacturing sector could mean that any competitive gains are quickly undone. So a fall in the exchange rate would improve competitiveness but this might only be short-lived if there were inflationary consequences. Further, if the currencies of some of Britain's major competitors depreciated (such as the euro), any competitive advantage gained would quickly be lost. A major issue is that the government has no direct control over the exchange rate, so this might not be a realistic policy to increase competitiveness. **b**

To make a more permanent improvement in Britain's competitiveness, other measures are likely to be necessary. An increase in spending on education and training might help. In particular, the government could improve the relevance of qualifications offered at school so that they are geared more particularly to the manufacturing sector. This is likely to result in a more productive, efficient workforce capable of producing goods at a lower average cost, so helping to enhance price competitiveness. A further benefit is that it is also likely to improve non-price competitiveness of UK goods, since a better trained workforce is more likely to produce goods of higher quality. However, this is very much a long-term factor that would take many years to filter through in terms of productivity gains. Also, it could be argued that the government is not the best body to invest

in training for future workers, as firms know far better what skills are required. Finally, it could be argued that there are dangers in training workers to participate in an industry that, as a result of deindustrialisation, is in terminal decline. This could result in structural unemployment later. **c**

Another policy might be for the government to promote investment by offering tax relief on investment. Extra machinery and capital equipment might help to increase productivity through capital deepening (i.e. increasing the amount of capital per worker). This would help to drive down costs and probably result in an increase in the quality of the goods produced, hence helping both price and non-price competitiveness. **d** However, again, this is a long-term policy involving a great degree of uncertainty on the firm's part as to whether it will result in competitive gains. At present, confidence among UK manufacturers is so low that they are unlikely to be willing to invest, as they are not certain that future profits will be sufficient to fund such investment. **e**

A further policy that the government could use to improve the competitiveness would be to subsidise the UK manufacturing sector. This would enable companies to lower prices and so improve competitiveness. However, there is likely to be a misallocation of resources because inefficient firms would remain in business: the resources used by those firms might be used more efficiently in other ways. **f**

The government could help to fund increased investment in infrastructure such as new roads, railways and internet speed and access. Investment in roads, for example, would help to reduce the unit costs of domestic businesses by reducing transport costs. It is also a way of attracting foreign direct investment from transnational companies. The technologies and working practices that they bring would help to improve the UK's competitiveness greatly. However, this strategy would be funded from tax revenues, which means that the government might be forced to raise taxes to fund these improvements to infrastructure. **g**

Overall, an increase in long-term competitiveness can only be achieved through a range of supply-side policies as outlined above. A depreciation of the exchange rate might bring a temporary improvement in competitiveness but this may not be sustained in the long run. On the other hand, if there is evidence that sterling is overvalued, then a depreciation in its value would help to improve price competitiveness. **h**

@ **25/30 marks awarded a** The answer begins by discussing the impact of exchange rate adjustment by correctly considering the effect of depreciation on the price of exports. However, there is no mention of the impact on import prices. **b** The remainder of the paragraph provides relevant evaluation of the improved price competitiveness of imports. **c** A sound discussion of the significance of education and training as a means of increasing productivity, which includes several evaluative comments. Diagrammatic analysis to show the impact of this supply-side policy could have been included. **d** The analysis of the possible impact of increased investment on productivity, costs and quality is very sound. **e** This sentence explains clearly why investment might not occur and so is good evaluation. **f** The policy on subsidising manufacturers is dubious because it may contravene WTO rules and conditions of EU membership. **g** Investment in infrastructure is related well to the possibility of attracting FDI and then followed by a brief but relevant evaluative comment. **h** A good concluding paragraph that reinforces some of the key points made earlier.

@ **Total score: 38/50 = grade B**

Data–response questions

Data–response question 3 **The economy of Nigeria**

Despite the global slump, congestion at Lagos, Nigeria's commercial capital, continues. The number of inbound containers has doubled in the past 3 years; so far in 2009 there has been no decline. Such is the crush in Lagos that getting cargo from ship to port to lorry still takes an average of 6 weeks.

Such blockages are nothing to celebrate but they indicate how 140 million Nigerians, despite being battered by a sharp fall in oil revenues and by an equally painful 20% devaluation of their currency, the naira, remain hungry for imports. Retailers tell a similar story. Coca-Cola plans to serve Nigerians over 2 billion bottles of sugary drinks this year, as it did last year. Proctor & Gamble, which sells nappies, washing powder etc. reports some slackening of growth but still expects the young and fast-growing population to push up consumer demand in the next few years. Mobile phone companies continue to boast about healthy sales of handsets and new armies of subscribers. Meanwhile, good hotels in Lagos still charge astronomical rates, building sites are crowded and vendors throng the streets as ever.

But like many poor countries, Nigeria has not escaped the global storm. It relies heavily on oil and gas exports, which provide more than 95% of all foreign currency earnings and most of the government's tax revenue. Both have crashed because of the tumbling price of oil, now at about $40 a barrel: more than $100 a barrel less than the peak in 2008. With nothing else to export — all those containers leave empty — Nigeria is especially vulnerable to fluctuating oil prices. Foreign direct investment, which flowed in a year or two ago, is flowing the other way. Most of it served the hydrocarbon industry but some foreign investors, especially Americans, had started to see Nigeria as an emerging market. A property bubble burst; the Nigerian Stock Exchange has tumbled by around 40% from its peak. Speculators and local banks are painfully out of pocket.

The government has responded by adopting an expansionary budget. Nigeria, along with Africa as a whole, should be spared outright recession. Sub-Saharan Africa's economies are expected to grow by roughly 3% in 2009, with Nigeria achieving a higher rate but not the 6% plus of recent years. This would barely match the rate of population growth. Economic reforms mean that Nigeria is fairly well placed to deal with a slowdown. Inflation, apart from food prices, is quite low. The government has paid off sizeable debts or been relieved of them. It also has ample foreign exchange reserves and has a special fund which will help to cushion public finances from the downturn. However, raising cash is getting harder: plans to sell $500m of bonds on the international market have been postponed.

Yet even if the global crisis has not hit Nigeria as hard as elsewhere, it is exposing some unresolved problems. The banks have looked vulnerable and have virtually

stopped lending to each other, partly because they had secured a large portion of their loans with equities which are now almost worthless.

Oil and gas production is also in bad shape: long Africa's biggest producer, Nigeria was overtaken by Angola in 2008. Production is dropping, in part because militants in the Niger delta kidnap workers and scare away oil firms. A new pipeline built to export gas to Ghana, Togo and Benin lies empty. Meanwhile, power cuts are common in Nigeria, which means that manufacturers must rely on expensive diesel generators. A law ordering the privatisation of some power stations has been reversed by the new government because of fears about corruption.

However, agriculture is a bright spot. Nigeria's lands are fertile and water, at least in the south, is plentiful. Local food and tobacco prices remain high compared with world prices, which should give farmers incentives.

Source: The Economist Newspapers Ltd, London (12 March 2009)

(a) 'Coca-Cola plans to serve Nigerians over 2 billion bottles of sugary drinks this year, as it did last year.' In view of the global downturn, how might the stability of sales of Coca-Cola be explained? (5 marks)

Since this is a quotation from the extract, it is important to use the material provided, which gives a key reason. Also, there is an opportunity to apply microeconomic concepts.

(b) Explain the implications of the bursting of the property bubble and the fall in share prices for the Nigerian economy. (8 marks)

Property and shares are examples of assets. In this case they have fallen value, which should signal that there is a negative wealth effect.

(c) Assess the likely effects of the 20% devaluation of the naira. (10 marks)

This is a straightforward question that demands a discussion of the implications of a reduction in the value of the Nigerian currency. A good answer would not focus solely on the impact on the current account of the balance of payments but consider the broader implications for the economy, for example, on economic growth, unemployment and inflation.

(d) Evaluate the significance of Nigeria's heavy dependence on oil exports. (12 marks)

Essentially, this is a question about primary product dependency but in this case the product is oil, which should be taken into account in the analysis and evaluation.

(e) In the light of the information provided, evaluate the prospects for the Nigerian economy. (15 marks)

In view of the question, it is important to use the information provided, which is plentiful, and then develop associated analysis by applying relevant economic concepts.

Student answer

(a) One factor which might explain the expected stability of sales of Coca-Cola is the 'young and fast-growing population'. This implies that any fall in demand associated with the global recession will be offset by rising demand from the increased size of population. **a**

Also, it could be that demand for Coca-Cola is income inelastic, i.e. a change in income would result in a significantly less than proportionate fall in demand. **b**

ⓔ **5/5 marks awarded a** The reason why sales of Coca-Cola are expected to remain stable is explained well, making good use of the extract. **b** The student applies and explains income elasticity of demand well.

(b) Property and shares are key assets. A reduction in their value is likely, therefore, to result in a negative wealth effect (i.e. as asset prices fall, people will feel less wealthy and, in turn, this will result in a fall in consumer spending as confidence declines). Some homeowners might find themselves in negative equity and so find it difficult to move. **a** On the other hand, if home ownership is low in Nigeria, the effects may not be significant.

The fall in share prices might imply a fall in business confidence, so making it more difficult for firms to raise money for investment. It could make Nigerian businesses more vulnerable to takeovers by foreign firms as they appear relatively cheap. **b**

ⓔ **4/8 marks awarded a** The student begins the answer well with a discussion of the negative wealth effect. **b** There is then an analysis of the impact on business confidence. However, to score highly, analysis of the broader effects on the Nigerian economy should have been considered, i.e. the fall in consumption and investment are components of aggregate demand and so the AD curve would shift to the left, causing a fall in real output and a fall in the price level. In turn, unemployment is likely to increase.

(c) A devaluation implies that the Nigerian economy has a fixed exchange rate, i.e. the value of the naira is fixed in relation to the dollar and other currencies. Nigeria's goods should become more competitive because a devaluation of the naira implies that its exports will appear cheaper abroad but imports will become more expensive. The devaluation should, therefore, lead to an increased demand for Nigeria's exports and a fall in demand for imports. This will cause aggregate demand to rise and real output to increase. **a**

There should also be an improvement in Nigeria's balance of payments on current account because Nigeria's goods will have become more competitive. However, this will only happen if the Marshall–Lerner condition is met, i.e. the price elasticity of demand for imports plus the price elasticity of demand for exports must be greater than 1. Further, the supply of Nigeria's exports must be elastic, i.e. exporters must be able to respond quickly to an increase in demand for their products. **b**

There is a danger that the higher price of imports could lead to cost-push inflation, i.e. if costs of imported raw materials rise, then this would cause production costs and prices to increase; this might then cause workers to demand wage increases which would result in a wage–price spiral. Consequently, the benefits of devaluation would be quickly lost. **c**

@ **6/10 marks awarded a** Devaluation is explained accurately. **b** There is some relevant evaluation in terms of the Marshall–Lerner condition and the elasticity of supply of exports. However, the student could have included more evaluation and reference to the J-curve. **c** AD/AS analysis could have been employed, with the relevant diagram showing the AD curve shifting to the right following an increase in exports and the AS curve shifting to the left following the cost-push inflationary pressures. In terms of evaluation, specific reference should also be made to the context: Nigeria being dependent on exports of primary products. Demand for these is likely to be inelastic and so export earnings could fall, following devaluation of the naira.

(d) A particular problem of oil dependence for Nigeria is that of price fluctuations. For example, oil prices have fallen by over $100 a barrel in less than a year. This causes big fluctuations in foreign currency earnings and makes it difficult for the oil companies to plan investment and output. **a**

There is a particular problem in the case of oil; namely, that the oil extractors are foreign owned and there appears to be considerable resentment towards them. As it states in the text: 'Production is dropping, in part, because militants in the Niger delta kidnap workers and scare away oil firms.' This might result in decreased investment in the future as companies look to other countries with greater political stability.

Ultimately, the oil will run out, so it will be necessary for Nigeria to diversify into other industries if it is to continue to grow. However, transnational companies might be deterred from investing in Nigeria, given the political instability. **b**

Nevertheless, oil is still significant as one of the world's key energy resources and Nigeria has benefited from foreign direct investment from companies such as Shell, which have helped to extract the oil. This FDI has benefited the financial account of the balance of payments and the subsequent exports have benefited the current account of the balance of payments, as well as being an important source of foreign currency with which to buy imported capital equipment and other manufactured goods. **c**

@ **6/12 marks awarded a** The student has made use of the information provided, explaining the significance of the price volatility of oil prices. **b** These two paragraphs explain two further problems of dependency on oil. **c** The last paragraph highlights positive impacts on the balance of payments. However, the significance for tax revenues and foreign currency earnings could have been examined further.

(e) Despite the current economic crisis, the Nigerian economy appears to be performing quite well. Imports are still booming, as evidenced by the log jam of boats trying to unload their goods at Lagos. Sales of luxury items, such as mobile phones, are booming; hotels are doing good trade, street vendors are busy and there is construction activity on building sites. However, there is some evidence that the growth of demand for items such as washing powder is slackening. Of more concern is that exports seem to be low, possibly resulting in a balance of payments deficit on current account that would cause a fall in aggregate demand and, therefore, a slower rate of economic growth. The reverse wealth effect of falling asset prices is likely to reinforce this fall in aggregate demand. **a**

Further, Nigeria's economy appears to be heavily dependent on primary products and, therefore, the prospects for the economy might not appear to be good. The Prebisch–Singer hypothesis suggests that the terms of trade (ratio of export prices to import prices) of a country dependent on primary goods will fall over time. The reason is that demand for most primary products is income inelastic, whereas the demand for manufactured goods, which must be imported, is income elastic. As world incomes rise over time, the prices of manufactured goods will increase relative to the prices of primary products. However, it is suggested in the passage that the prices of food and tobacco 'remain high' and it is likely that oil prices will recover, once there is the prospect of world recovery. **b**

Nevertheless, the Nigerian macroeconomy is fundamentally sound: the economy is expected to grow by 6%, twice as fast as other African countries; inflation is low and the government has paid off much of its debt. Also, it has adequate foreign exchange reserves and funds available to deal with a deterioration in the public finances which might arise from the downturn in the economy. The agricultural sector is also performing well since it has fertile land. **c**

However, there are problems facing the economy, not least that FDI has now turned negative, suggesting that there is capital flight. **d** This could result in inadequate savings to fund future investment — deemed as essential for growth according to the Harrod–Domar model. Further, the banking system is paralysed, with banks unwilling to lend to each other and to customers. This problem, along with the negative outflows, would result in a fall in aggregate demand (because investment is a component of *AD*) and in long-run aggregate supply, since the productive capacity of the country would decline. **e**

There is also the problem of interruptions in power supplies that could disrupt production and slow economic growth. Also, corruption appears to be a problem, since proposed privatisations have been cancelled. This might deter future foreign direct investment.

ⓔ **13/15 marks awarded a** Good use of the information provided, followed by pertinent evaluative comments. **b** A good summary of the significance of the Prebisch–Singer hypothesis. **c** The positive prospects for the Nigerian economy are explained well in this paragraph. **d** The concept of capital flight could have been defined and its significance explained. **e** An *AS/AD* diagram could have been included to illustrate the effects of the outflow of investment.

ⓔ **Total score: 34/50 = grade C**

Data–response question 4 **The vulnerability of sterling**

Since late 2007, sterling has fallen significantly against most currencies, not least against the dollar (see Figure A).

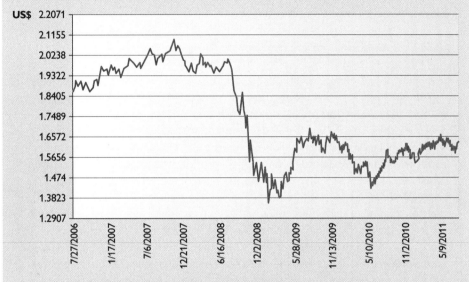

Figure A US dollar to pound sterling exchange rate

Source: www.indexmundi.com/xrates/graph.aspx?c1=USD&c2=GBP&days=

Sterling looks especially vulnerable in the harsh new world that has dawned after the credit crisis. One worry is that the public finances are in a mess, which might undermine confidence among foreign investors, who hold a third of all gilt-edged securities. Another is that Britain, with its big financial services sector, is Iceland writ large.

There is something in both concerns but not much. The Treasury's forecast for the budget deficit, due to rise in 2009 to 8% of GDP, is dismal. Yet Britain's public debt compares favourably with that of other large economies. As for the notion that Britain is a bigger Iceland, whose currency crashed with its banks, this misses several points. For one thing, size matters. Iceland has a population of 300,000 compared with Britain's 60 million; its national output and fiscal resources are commensurately smaller. More important, Iceland's banking liabilities in mid-2008 were almost ten times the size of its GDP, according to the OECD. Britain's were 4.7% times output, somewhat higher than in the euro area (3.5%) but lower than in Switzerland (6.8%).

Britain's relatively high ratio reflects the City's longstanding role as an international financial centre. The foreign banks that cluster there account for over half of all banking liabilities in Britain and two-thirds of those in foreign currency. By contrast, Iceland's own banks accounted for all its banking liabilities, and most of these were in foreign currency.

The fall in the pound may have been disconcertingly large but it makes an overdue adjustment after a long period in which sterling was overpriced. According to the OECD, sterling's purchasing power parities against the dollar and the euro are $1.590 and €1.30 respectively. This suggests that the pound is now close to its underlying value against the dollar and about 15% below its long-term value against the euro.

Sterling's slide has been greeted with dismay by British tourists, but their pain is part of the remedy for Britain's economic ills. The pound's fall is similarly benefiting British exporters. As long as their overseas markets are also suffering from the global downturn, the pound's fall is not enough to make up for weakening foreign demand. But it does make the exports they can sell more profitable and encourages them to build up their presence abroad.

Advocates of British membership of the euro found it difficult to make their case while sterling was thriving. Now the pound is falling, they are finding a readier audience. Yet monetary sovereignty is all the more crucial when the economy is in trouble. The Bank of England has been able to cut interest rates below those in the euro area for the first time since the single currency started in 1999. This, in turn, has pushed sterling down — a stimulus all the more welcome since monetary policy is less effective than usual because the banks are unwilling to lend.

The weaker pound will help not just to soften the blow of recession but also to create a basis for subsequent recovery that will be necessarily less reliant on consumers. The inflationary impact of sterling's slide will be countered by the collapse in commodity prices and the contraction in economic activity.

Source: adapted from The *Economist*, 20 December 2008

(a) With reference to Figure A, explain how exchange rates are determined under a system of floating exchange rates. (5 marks)

☺ This question demands an understanding of how the forces of supply and demand may be applied to exchange rates. Given the reference to Figure A, it is important to include a specific data reference.

(b) Explain reasons why sterling might have been over-priced for a long period of time. (8 marks)

☺ At least two reasons should be identified and explained in order to provide an effective response to this question, one of which is implicit in the extract.

(c) Assess the reasons why 'sterling looks especially vulnerable'. (10 marks)

☺ This question demands an understanding of the reasons why the value of sterling may fall against other currencies, together with some evaluation.

(d) Assess the likely effect of the fall in the value of the pound on Britain's tourist industry. (12 marks)

ⓔ To provide a full answer there should be a discussion of the impact on both British citizens travelling abroad and foreigners travelling to the UK. Further, the answer should focus not just on the implications for the balance of payments but on the broader effects on the tourist industry in Britain. The command word 'assess' indicates that evaluation is required.

(e) In view of the state of the British economy, evaluate the arguments in favour of Britain's membership of the euro. (15 marks)

ⓔ It is important not just to write out the standard arguments for and against Britain's membership of the euro but to address the first part of the question relating to the state of the British economy.

Student answer

(a) Under a system of floating exchange rates, the value of a currency is determined by the supply and demand for that currency on the foreign exchange market. Figure A shows a fall in the value of the pound sterling against the dollar from nearly $2.12 in November 2007 to just below $1.38 in March 2009. **a** This could be explained by a decrease in demand for sterling or an increase in the supply of sterling. Demand might have fallen as a result of a loss in confidence in the UK economy, while supply might have risen as investors withdrew their savings from the UK economy associated with the fall in interest rates. **b**

ⓔ **5/5 marks awarded a** There is an accurate explanation of how the value of the currency is determined, with an appropriate reference to the data. **b** The last part of the response provides reasons why the value of the pound might have fallen, which ensures maximum marks.

(b) The extract states that UK interest rates were higher than those of euro countries until recently. This would make it attractive for foreign individuals and companies to place surplus funds in UK banks. This would increase the demand for sterling on the foreign exchange markets and so cause the value of the pound to increase. **a**

Another factor is that, until recently, the British economy has been relatively strong, especially compared with economies such as Italy and France. The confidence generated by this strength of the economy gave people an incentive to hold sterling in preference to other currencies. **b**

The UK, with its flexible labour market and growing economy, was very successful in attracting foreign direct investment — more so than other European economies. This also created a demand for sterling and so helped to maintain a high value for sterling. **c**

ⓔ **6/8 marks awarded a** This first point on relative interest rates could have been illustrated with a supply and demand diagram showing a rightward shift in the demand curve for sterling and an increase in its value. **b** It might have been better to have explained why the strength of the British economy made it attractive *for foreigners* to hold sterling. **c** It is worth noting that FDI causes an inflow of foreign currency into the financial account of the balance of payments.

(c) Two factors that might explain why sterling looks especially vulnerable are the poor state of Britain's public finances and the significance of the financial sector.

    Britain's public sector borrowing is expected to be £175 billion in the year 2009–10 and to remain at these high levels for several years. Meanwhile, public sector debt could reach £1 trillion in the next few years. However, absolute numbers are not very meaningful. Borrowing as a proportion of GDP needs to be considered: the fiscal deficit is expected to be about 12% of GDP, while public sector debt is expected to rise to about 79% of GDP. These are high proportions historically and they may cause a loss of confidence in the British economy and its ability to sell sufficient gilt-edged securities to cover the debts. In turn, this explains why people may be unwilling to hold sterling. However, the extract shows that Britain's situation is significantly better than that of Iceland, which has a much smaller population and much smaller GDP. **a**

    The other factor is Britain's financial services sector, which probably accounts for about 9% of GDP. Obviously, this has been seriously hit by the financial crisis but now the recession is affecting most parts of the economy. **b** With regard to banking liabilities, these amount to 4.7 times output, about two thirds of which were in foreign currency, whereas Iceland's banking liabilities amounted to 10 times output, most of which were in foreign currency. In this context, Britain's position does not seem so severe. However, compared with the euro area, Britain looks more exposed to a downturn in the financial sector, so this factor may also explain why the value of the pound depreciated and may depreciate further. **c**

ⓔ **8/10 marks awarded a** A good point making appropriate use of the data, with one evaluative comment at the end. **b** A relevant point that helps to explain why sterling looks vulnerable. **c** Some relevant evaluative comments are made for both points, but these should have been developed more fully. For example, the arguments could be prioritised: many would argue that Britain's public finances are in such a poor state that Britain might be forced to borrow from the IMF if it is unable to sell enough gilt-edged securities to foreign investors. This factor, therefore, is likely to be the most significant in explaining why the pound might fall in value.

(d) The fall in the value of the pound will make it more expensive for British tourists to travel abroad because a pound will buy fewer dollars or units of other currencies. Therefore, demand for foreign holidays is likely to decrease and more British people will take holidays at home. However, there is some evidence that the British are unwilling to give up their foreign holidays, suggesting that demand may be income inelastic. **a**

    In contrast, foreigners will find it cheaper to take holidays in this country because they will receive more pounds for each unit of their currency. Figure A shows that the pound has fallen at least 25% against the dollar and the euro. Consequently, the demand for holidays in Britain will increase. However, foreigners may be deterred from holidaying in the UK because of its reputation for poor weather, expensive hotels and poor infrastructure. Also, demand for

holidays tends to be income elastic at times of world recession; therefore, demand might fall more than proportionately relative to income. **b**

Overall, the British tourist industry should benefit from rising demand. This should lead to an increase in revenues and profits but much will depend on the extent of the increase in demand. Employment in the tourist industry is also likely to increase. However, most of it is likely to be seasonal and low skilled. **c**

ⓔ **10/12 marks awarded a** A good introduction that considers the cost implications of a fall in the value of sterling, together with an evaluative comment at the end of the paragraph. **b** It is good practice to apply concepts such as income elasticity of demand in this context. **c** This paragraph considers some of the broader implications and includes some relevant evaluation.

(e) The dramatic fall in the value of the pound has given supporters of the euro an important argument: that of greater stability. Businesses might argue that a more stable exchange rate would enable firms to plan investment and output more easily. Further, it would make budgeting more predictable, e.g. import costs would be more stable, as would revenues received from exports.

In the current situation of macroeconomic uncertainty, being a member of the euro might be more attractive for transnational companies considering foreign direct investment. It is possible that euro membership might be a crucial factor in making such an investment decision. **a**

Another argument in favour of British membership of the euro is that at least 60% of British exports are to countries that have adopted the euro, so a closer link with these countries might appear to be a logical development. It also means that transaction costs are eliminated, i.e. there are no costs involved in changing currencies when trade between two countries occurs. **b**

On the other hand, retaining the pound has enabled Britain to follow an independent monetary policy. It is stated in the extract that British interest rates have fallen below those in the euro zone for the first time since 1999, when the euro started. This illustrates how the Bank of England is able to respond to Britain's economic needs without the necessity to consider those of other countries. However, monetary policy has proved to offer limited value at times of financial crisis, when banks are unwilling to lend to each other. **c**

Further, the exchange rate of the pound has fallen significantly (about 25%), giving Britain a valuable competitive advantage when a recovery occurs. This depreciation in the value of sterling will make exports cheaper and imports more expensive, so making British goods more competitive. This should help to create export-led growth without inflationary consequences, since commodity prices are likely to remain relatively low until there is a significant improvement in the state of the world economy. **d**

ⓔ 13/15 marks awarded **a** The first two paragraphs are based on the idea of greater stability, which could stimulate both domestic investment and FDI. While this is a valid point, it could have been evaluated, e.g. Britain has not suffered a serious loss of FDI by not being a member of the eurozone. **b** The elimination of transactions costs is frequently cited as a major benefit of joining the eurozone but these costs are relatively insignificant, an evaluative point that could have been made. **c** The ability to follow an independent monetary policy by not being part of the eurozone is often seen as a benefit but the limitations of monetary policy could have been developed more fully. **d** Again, some evaluation of this point could have been included, e.g. if there is slow growth in other countries then export-led growth might not occur.

ⓔ **Total score: 42/50 = grade A**

Knowledge check answers

1 A rise in oil prices would cause costs of production and transport to rise, causing a leftward shift in the AS curve. In turn, this would cause a rise in price level and fall in real output. As a net importer of oil, the UK would face an increase in the value of imports (since the demand for oil is price inelastic). This would cause a fall in AD and a further fall in real output.

2 Banks might be charging considerably higher interest rates on loans than the Bank of England's base rate. Further, banks may be unwilling to lend if they consider the risks of non-repayment to be too great. A lack of confidence might mean that firms and consumers are unwilling to borrow.

3 It is very likely that public finances would deteriorate: automatic stabilisers mean that government expenditure on social benefits for the unemployed would increase while tax revenues would fall (not only from incomes but also from a reduction in revenues from expenditure taxes e.g. VAT and from corporation tax).

4 Non-excludability, i.e. it is impossible to prevent people from consuming a product once it is provided; and non-rivalrous, i.e. consumption by one person does not limit consumption by others.

5 Investment is likely to fall because interest rates will be higher so causing a rise in the cost of borrowing, which would deter investment.

6 It would cause the value of the multiplier to fall because leakages have risen.

7 It will reduce it because less is now being sacrificed by taking an extra hour of leisure. Therefore, higher income tax rates may be a disincentive to work.

8 The fiscal deficit implies that public expenditure is greater than tax revenues in a particular year whereas the National Debt is the accumulation of government borrowing from previous years.

9 It could limit globalisation if higher transport costs make it less likely for firms to relocate production plants or service activities abroad.

10 Those countries with very low savings ratios are more likely to have current account deficits on the balance of payments because a low savings ratio implies a high propensity to consume, with an associated high level of imports.

11 According to the law of comparative advantage, specialisation will lead to increased output. For consumers, there should be more choice and lower prices and firms should benefit from larger markets and economies of scale.

12 The size of the tariff as well as the price elasticity of demand and domestic price elasticity of supply. If demand and supply are both price elastic, the tariff will be more effective in reducing imports.

13 Free trade between member countries.

14 Various factors could be responsible, including: relatively low unit labour costs; relatively high productivity; a relatively low inflation rate; undervaluation of the currency; non-price competitive advantages such as design, quality and reliability of the product.

15 This could result in a loss of confidence in the currency, so causing its value to fall. However, if defaulting countries left the eurozone, leaving just the strong members, then the euro would probably rise in value.

16 The current account would deteriorate, i.e. the deficit would get larger since the Marshall–Lerner condition had not been fulfilled.

17 That country's international competitiveness would decline since a relatively lower productivity rate implies that its unit costs of production would rise relative to its competitors.

18 The Lorenz curve would move further away from the 45° line.

19 Many hard commodities such as cotton and iron ore are raw materials used to manufacture goods used for everyday purposes whereas soft commodities such as wheat and rice are part of the staple diets of many people and their demand would rise less than proportionately to a rise in income.

20 The marginal propensity to save is likely to be low because poor people have to spend a high proportion of their incomes simply to provide for their basic human needs.

21 It would increase because there would be more dependants, i.e. those under 16 and over 65, relative to the number of workers.

22 FDI is undertaken by transnational companies with the aim of making a profit for shareholders whereas aid refers to grants or loans at less than the market rate of interest (called concessional loans) given to developing countries by governments, international organisations or non-government organisations.

23 This refers to the interest paid on loans. In the case of a government, it means that it would have less money available to spend on public services.

24 There is a danger that countries whose debts have been cancelled will follow policies that result in their building up further debts in the future.

25 This states that, when successive units in a variable factor of production are added to fixed factors, the marginal product will eventually decrease.

26 These include: exploitation of labour and the environment; employment possibly being in low-skilled, poorly-paid jobs; repatriation of profits to shareholders in the developed country where the TNC is based; disruption to the economy if the TNC withdraws its investment.

27 If individuals have no property rights then they will not have any collateral to secure a loan from a bank to start a business.

28 Producers in developed countries may have monopsony power, enabling them to drive down the prices which they pay for goods from producers in developing countries.

29 It has loaned money to countries such as Greece, Ireland and Portugal in an attempt to prevent their governments defaulting on their debts. Strict conditions are attached to these loans, for example, austerity measures to reduce fiscal deficits.

Edexcel A2 Economics

PHILIP ALLAN

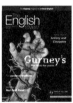
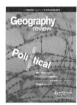